Considering
Filipinos

The InterAct Series

GEORGE W. RENWICK, Series Editor

Other books in the series:
WITH RESPECT TO THE JAPANESE
UNDERSTANDING ARABS
GOOD NEIGHBORS: INTERACTING WITH THE MEXICANS
A COMMON CORE: THAIS AND AMERICANS

Considering Filipinos

THEODORE GOCHENOUR

INTERCULTURAL PRESS, INC.

For information, contact:
Intercultural Press, Inc.
P.O. Box 700
Yarmouth, ME 04096 USA

Library of Congress No. 90-055633
ISBN 0-933662-89-0

Library of Congress Cataloging-in-Publication Data
Gochenour, Theodore.
    Considering Filipinos / by Theodore Gochenour.
        p.   cm.
    Includes bibliographical references.
    ISBN 0-933662-89-0
    1. National characteristics, Philippine. 2. National characteristics, American. 3. Philippines—Civilization. 4. United States—Civilization—1970- I. Title
    DS665.G63   1990
    303.48'2599073—dc20   90-55633
                                                                CIP

Printed in the United States of America.

Contents

Acknowledgments

Grateful thanks are due to Mrs. Daisy Suministrado, colleague and friend, for her invaluable assistance in preparing this book, and to my wife, Yolanda Pareja Cabiluna Gochenour, for being my "in-house" cultural advisor and teacher.

The cover and chapter opening illustrations depict the **sarimanok** bird. Originally part of the folk tradition of the Maranao people in Lanao province, the sarimanok bird is now an accepted symbol of Filipino culture.

Preface

The close relationship between the U.S. and the Philippines has been of long duration and has had both its bright and its dark moments. Despite stresses that have developed in the post-Marcos era, relations are likely to remain close for some time into the future. The ties that bind the two countries are too strong to be easily broken.

But such ties cannot be taken for granted. The history of relations between nations is fraught with the consequences of misbegotten assumptions about motivations, thought patterns, and feelings. It is the intent of the *InterAct* Series to illuminate the intercultural side of transnational interactions by exploring differences in perception, ways of thinking, styles of communication, and customary behaviors. An InterAct explains what happens when individuals who have grown up in contrasting cultures meet, eat, joke, argue, negotiate, and cooperate with one another. It probes the feelings people from different cultures have about each other, their expectations, the effect their interactions have, and the way what is said and done by one embarrasses, frustrates, motivates, impresses, or angers the other. It attempts to predict the outcome of encounters between cultures. It offers advice and guidelines for the wary traveler and sojourner abroad; it makes clear what one must do to become a clever competitor or a trusted colleague and friend.

In the sensitive, often charged atmosphere that can develop among Filipinos and Americans when they deal with each other, understanding the forces at work and the cross-cultural dynamics within their interactions may in the future be a *sine qua non* to maintaining the special relationship that has existed for so long. No one is more qualified to contribute to that understanding than Ted Gochenour. He has spent much of his professional life working abroad as an educator and consultant. For many years he served as vice president of the Experiment in International Living, an organization with a long history and exceptional reputation in the field of international educational exchange. During the mid-1980s, he was director of the Southeast Asian Refugee Center in Bataan, Philippines. There he married a Filipino and pursued the observations, research, and extensive contact with local people that prepared him to produce this work. As this book goes to press, Ted is living and working in Nepal.

We are pleased to add this volume to the Intercultural Press's *InterAct* Series.

George W. Renwick
Editor, *InterAct* Series

Foreword

When one is asked to consider Filipinos, the most probable response is to ask, "What is Filipino?" Spread out over a 7,100-island archipelago and inhabiting some five hundred of the islands, Filipinos speak eighty-seven languages and dialects. As the United States is the major multicultural society of the West, the Philippines can be considered its counterpart in the East. No other country in Asia is as ethnically diverse. In any urban center one has to be at least bilingual to survive. Yet, whether their ancestry be Malay, Indochinese, Negroid, European, or Chinese, contemporary history has shown that the citizens of the Philippines rise above diversity and unite to become the eternal Filipino.

Residing on islands that dot the western rim of the Pacific Ocean, Filipinos have always been travelers. Two million of them live abroad—in Europe, the Middle East, the Americas, and in Asia—lending their expertise as builders, physicians, educators, and musicians. Most of the ships that sail the seven seas will have at least one Filipino seaman on board. In leading hotels around the world, one will often be waited on by Filipinos. A patient in an American hospital is likely to be assisted back to health by a Filipino nurse or doctor. Filipino expertise has already reached the moon—in the form of the lunar module, which was designed by a

Filipino engineer. Everywhere, monuments to man's ingenuity—dams, airports, freeways, and canals—have been built with Filipino help.

We are grateful to Theodore Gochenour for having written this book about Filipinos. I urge you to read it. You will probably like it—and us.

Raul S. Manglapus
Secretary for Foreign Affairs
Republic of the Philippines

Good Morning, Manila

There you are, standing twenty stories above Roxas Boulevard, watching bumper-to-bumper traffic down below. Just beyond is one of the world's perfect harbors, Manila Bay. Last evening, you took a taxi which stayed, generally, on the right-hand side of the road, and you carried on a conversation with the driver in English. You passed stores selling Apple and IBM computers, Levis, and Westinghouse refrigerators before stopping to buy some Colgate toothpaste and Old Spice shaving cream. You now turn on the TV in your hotel room and "Good Morning, Manila" is on the air.

The signs are intelligible, the names of streets are pronounceable, an English-language newspaper is slipped under your hotel door, courtesy of the management. There is a coffee shop around the corner where you can get ham and eggs for less than half the price as in the U.S. The maid has a sister who is a nurse in Des Moines, and the father of the desk clerk just retired from a military career—with the U.S. Navy. There are two bookshops within walking distance, each filled with American titles. The people are polite and seem much friendlier than they do in some countries you could name. What could be difficult about getting along in *this* country?

For the American visiting or touring the Philippines, the answer to that question can easily be "not much." It is quite possible to meet Filipinos, see something of the country, and come away with the feeling of having interacted successfully and pleasantly with a

1

culture different enough to be charming and familiar enough to be comfortable. For many Americans—and Filipinos—that represents achievement enough. They may feel no need to probe beneath the outer shell of a passing relationship to see what cultural realities may lie within.

For some travelers, however, and certainly for the American working on a day-to-day basis with Filipinos, the answer may well be "quite a lot." Somehow, tensions rise or feelings get hurt or productivity drops off. Anger, even violence, may suddenly appear. The familiar and congenial can often be deceptive—obscuring profound differences. Ultimately, these differences must be seen and understood—on both sides—as problems, or as opportunities for understanding and communication.

Between the Republic of the Philippines and the United States a special relationship exists—one with emotional and historical ties closer perhaps than the U.S. shares with any nation other than Canada and Great Britain. This relationship commenced in betrayal, war, and occupation at the beginning of this century. Four decades of colonialism followed. With the close of World War II and the full independence of the Philippines in 1946, a new relationship began. Nevertheless, American strategic and economic interests have maintained a dominant role in Philippine development and politics, and American popular culture continues to have a powerful effect on Filipino lifestyles, language, and aspirations.

Filipinos tend to have a fair knowledge of the United States. Coverage of events in the U.S. on the TV news is not only commonplace, it hardly feels more foreign than would a broadcast originating in Hawaii to an American listener. Ask an educated Filipino to name the states, and the list will be impressive. Ask when the Pilgrims landed, and most likely he or she will name the year 1620.

On the other side of the relationship, however, Americans would be hard-pressed to identify more than one of the Philippine islands or come up with the name of a single province. Most would doubtless find it difficult to believe that the European presence in the Philippines began a century before the Pilgrims got on the boat. Older Americans might associate the name Bataan with the country, recalling the infamous Death March in 1942. The name Admiral Dewey may resonate dimly for those who got through that chapter in their high school history book. Others may recall the 1950s, when President Magsaysay seemed to receive favorable attention in the American press.

Since 1984 we have had more reason to be aware of the Philippines. The demise of the Marcos regime and evening news coverage of "People Power" have brought the Philippines into American living rooms and consciousness and touched our hearts with its struggle for democracy. News coverage has focused on some of the country's problems, particularly violence, coup attempts, and insurgency; less so on the economic and social problems festering behind the camera. For many Americans today, understanding of the Philippines begins, and ends, with a woman dressed in yellow, Cory Aquino. For numerous others, however, who have served in the armed forces, traveled, or worked there, the Republic of the Philippines is a special place, and Filipinos are people with whom Americans can communicate, live among, share goals, and achieve warm understanding.

What that amounts to, in practice, depends upon the American and the Filipino concerned. Just as there are numerous American attitudes, behaviors, values, and styles of living, so are there Filipino. The Filipino in a Manila nightclub is not necessarily any more a representative of the Philippines than is the woman presiding over a small *sari-sari* store in Davao. The American traveling to the Philippines would do well to start with the realization that tremendous contrasts abound within Filipino society. The attitudes and behaviors of upper-class, urban Filipinos are one thing. Those of fishermen on the South China Sea beaches are another. The ideas and objectives of a group of radical university students and those of a high school teacher in San Fernando with a mortgage to meet are likely to be equally divergent.

The aim of the following chapters is to provide a practical base for understanding the Philippines and its people, without getting into scholarly exactness and refinement. More specifically, the aim is to examine those cultural traits, both American and Filipino, which either help or hinder the process of interaction between the two peoples. An American traveler or sojourner should start by recognizing that there are at least two realities to confront: the visible Philippines and the one lying as a foundation under that. The first is normally quite agreeable to Americans and in many ways is familiar, warm, and welcoming. The second may be harder to perceive since the reasons why Filipinos act in one way or another or have the attitudes or ideas they do may be difficult for them to explain. Like other people around the world, Filipinos tend to assume that those reasons are self-evident to everyone.

To the extent possible, our discussion addresses a sort of "main-stream" Filipino culture. Necessarily, this truncates the reality of a richly diverse society. Without quibbling over definitions of interest mainly to specialists, it is possible to accept that generalizations are sometimes useful. If the American traveler or visitor remembers that exceptions likely exist to every statement found here, then all will be well.

The U.S. and the Philippines:
Friends, Foes, Family?

Geography created the base on which Filipino society is founded. It accounts for the predominance of the Malay stock, the nature of the country's languages, and many of its enduring cultural characteristics. A glance at the map explains something of the early historical impact of adjacent cultures—principally Chinese—on the Philippines through centuries of trade and settlement, long before the "discovery" of the islands by the Europeans.

A map conveys little, however, about many of the defining elements of Filipino culture and society today. The presence of a significant Muslim minority in the country, thousands of miles from Mecca, results more from historical expansionism than convenience of geography. Similarly, many of the beliefs, lifestyles, aspirations, and cultural traits of the modern Filipino owe their origins not to geographically close neighbors but to lands on the other side of the earth.

This archipelago in a corner of the Pacific has been a place where the indigenous has been heavily influenced by the foreign. Neither history nor geography permitted the Filipinos time to consolidate their parochial and isolated strands into a culture integrated enough to absorb or repel outside pressures and influences. Early Filipinos, who were seafarers and slash-and-burn farmers for the most part, were fragmented into small tribal units and cut off from each other either by water or difficult terrain. There may have been more large-scale social organization at an early date than is commonly believed, but the regional divisions and linguistic differences, which endure to the present, point toward long-established separateness of one area from another. More advanced cultures came as traders and, to some extent, settlers. The regional name of the group of central islands, Visayan, may trace its origins to the Sanskrit word for the merchant caste. Chinese traders and settlers arrived by A.D. 1000, initiating a profound influence on Filipino culture that is still evident today. Arab and Persian traders visited the Philippines well before the introduction of Islam. The founding and Islamification of Malacca in 1414 spread the influence of Islam among Malay peoples, and it soon became widely established throughout the southern Philippine islands.

In the sixteenth century, with the arrival of the Spanish to colonize and convert, the concept of a geographical unit called the "Filipinas" emerged, named in honor of Philip II, King of Spain. The Europeans also brought with them the idea of owning a territory thousands of miles from home and inhabited by people culturally and racially different from themselves. The Spanish stamped upon the Filipino culture and consciousness some of its most enduring characteristics. Hispanic Catholicism became dominant in the country. Fine arts, dress, dance, cuisine, and customs were influenced or modified. In addition to visible cultural impact, the centuries of Spanish rule left Filipinos with a legacy of attitudes that are firmly imbedded in the society: an equation of light skin with status, the identification of foreign with authority and indigenous with inferiority, and a conception of officialdom as a system serving its own ends, not those of the people.

The arrival of the Americans on the scene ninety years ago replaced one form of colonialism with another. None of the attitudinal legacies of the Spanish were removed by U.S. rule although Americans saw themselves as bestowers of education, public health, development, and democracy to their "little brown brothers." Most Americans have no knowledge of the bitter and bloody campaign the U.S. waged to overcome Filipino resistance in the early years of this century. At least a quarter of a million Filipino lives were lost. Like others, Americans tend to view history selectively. The arrival of an American fleet in Manila Bay in 1898, in the context of the Spanish-American War, may be one of those dates we distantly recall. The brutality in the ten years which followed never found a place in American high school history texts. A significant percentage of Americans today would probably be surprised to learn that the United States was once a colonial power.

For Filipinos, colonialism is a much clearer reality. The legacy of a history of external domination and influence remains potent in Filipino life and thought. Filipino culture today is a rich mixture of foreign and indigenous elements, a composite built up over centuries. Much of what was once extraneous in origin feels completely "right" and "Filipino" today. Some elements, however, are being scrutinized more and more critically by Filipino scholars, particularly the detrimental influences on Filipino attitudes and values resulting from colonialism. Four decades of independence have seen the emergence of a struggling but growing national awareness throughout the islands. Despite divisive regional identifications and even separatist movements among Muslims, Filipinos today have a stronger sense of national identity and share more in common than at any time in their history.

The cultural traits of a people are rooted in the history which has molded them. Filipinos and Americans share some decades together, but this period of time amounts to only a small fraction of the quite different histories which the two countries have experienced. Despite this difference, however, both cherish a heritage of many significant ideas and values rooted in Euro-Christian ethics. In addition, they both espouse certain ideals about democratic government, the value of education, freedom of the press, and personal liberty. Filipinos have a decidedly Western orientation, to the extent that "Asian-ness" is not a common identifying description among them.

Nevertheless, despite centuries of colonialism, Filipinos never allowed themselves to become carbon copies of their rulers. Although outward appearances may suggest otherwise at times, Filipino social and cultural characteristics contrast quite sharply with those of mainstream America. A number of beliefs, values, and ways of dealing with day-to-day life which Filipinos consider normal would feel strange or curious to many Americans. Filipinos, like any other people, hold dear those things which they feel are deeply distinctive about their culture. This is true even if the individual Filipino may be entirely capable of, and comfortable with, foreign modes of interaction. For example, the adaptability and the strongly rooted cultural norm of seeking consensus and good feeling among themselves can lead foreigners to charge Filipinos with being two-faced. Outwardly, one behavior is exhibited; inwardly, reservations are privately held. Americans may assume that similarities with Filipinos in dress, language, and behavior imply equal similarities in the way they think and feel and in the perspective they have on their relationship. There is, however, a Filipino "mask" which presents both to other Filipinos and to foreigners the outward appearance one wishes to convey. This may take the form, for example, of trying to look financially better off than is actually the case, or the mask may conceal anger, sorrow, or embarrassment behind an outwardly tranquil expression. Such management of the outward self owes some of its origin to the dual historical need among Filipinos to understand, accommodate to, placate, or oppose the overwhelming power foreigners have exercised in their lives while at the same time preserving what is essentially Filipino in themselves.

The fact that Americans are largely ignorant of the Philippines and its people is, itself, a factor affecting understanding and communication. Beyond being only dimly aware of the historical connections between the United States and the Philippines, visiting Americans are likely to have no more than a rudimentary knowledge of the geography, ethnic mix, languages, and cultural traits of the country. The Filipinos they meet, however, usually have a storehouse of information—and misinformation—about the United States. The initial imbalance in understanding gets even more complicated. The Filipinos will not *expect* Americans to know much about the Philippines. The Americans may hardly be embarrassed at their lack of knowledge or feel any need to take corrective measures. The Filipinos, however, feel chagrined at their lack of knowledge—of English, or about the States—thinking that they should be informed, particularly when dealing with an American.

Subtly and profoundly, lingering effects of a colonial relationship endure. In some ways, the colonial heritage may be less exploitative than preemptive: by establishing what is important to know and to think about. Schools in the U.S. still devote more attention to the doings of little England than to makers of history across the English Channel, not to mention the sagas of empires in Asia, with territories larger than all of Europe. Similarly, Filipino education includes considerably more focus on the United States than on neighboring countries of the Pacific. Years after independence, Filipino school children were still learning the American Pledge of Allegiance and studying American writers and poets, civics, and history. American schools, by contrast, have never considered knowledge of the Philippines to be particularly necessary.

One result of this historical relationship between the Philippines and the United States is the pleasant sensation of familiarity visiting Americans experience upon arrival in the country. They are greeted by signs advertising American products, they find English widely spoken, and, more subtly, they enjoy a status and receptivity perhaps unique in their travels. For Filipinos, America is the land of power, glamour, wealth, and opportunity. Even if the traveler tells them about the poverty, unemployment, and poor living conditions that exist in the U.S., Filipinos have trouble believing it, given their own difficulties. They figure that what is lacking in the Philippines will be abundant across the sea. At work here is not so much Filipino naivete, though there is some of that, but a persistent feeling buried in decades of tutelage that the U.S. ought to be all of the things they imagine and dream about.

The visitor, however, may also find an unpleasant side, again founded in the history of Philippine-American relations. While pre-World War II colonialism is not a problem of general concern, there are contemporary aspects of the relationship which do matter a great deal to many Filipinos: for example, American support for the repressive and corrupt regime of Ferdinand Marcos (1972-1986); the presence of the U.S. military bases at Subic Bay and Clark Field; and the effect of American decisions and agreements, such as the sugar quota or equal parity rights, on the economy and on Philippine autonomy. Some Filipinos hold strongly negative views of the U.S., holding it responsible for impeding or distorting Philippine development, exploiting the country economically, imposing consumerist values, dominating the modes of popular entertainment, and breaking agreements when it is in the interest of the U.S. to do so—in short, acting as an intruder who has granted independence to the residents but has never left the house. The observant American may see support for this view in the fact that development in the Philippines contrasts so poorly with that of many other countries in Asia and the Pacific.

These concerns are expressed more frequently and openly today than ever before. Obviously, they have an impact—however politely masked—on interaction between Filipinos and Americans. They help to form the matrix in which understanding is either reached or not, in which cultural expectations clash or find accommodation. What the American eventually detects, after being among Filipinos for a while, are subtle love/hate feelings toward the United States, fascination for things American existing side by side with fear and distrust.

Thus, the relationship does not start on an equal footing. Among Americans, for example, neither the experience of having been colonial subjects of the British nor of being a colonial power seems to weigh significantly on patterns of thinking and acting. For Filipinos, however, the experience of twice having been colonial subjects has had a powerful effect on the nature of the society. Filipinos sometimes explain aspects of their behavior—the resistance to or subverting of legal authority, for instance—by referring to their experience under colonial domination, usually Spanish. After all, there were 350 years of it. There is no doubt that the Spanish colonial heritage is more profound than the American. Its effects are felt on a basic level—affecting family relationships, religious beliefs, socials customs, and ways of dealing with authority and power. Interestingly, it imparted a somewhat Mexican flavor to Filipino life, traceable to the fact that the Philippines were administered for a long time as a division of the Mexican department of the Spanish empire.

Americans may find other evidence of an underlying inequality in the relationship, rooted in differing colonial roles. White Americans may be troubled by the fact that the color of their skin turns out to be rather important in the Philippines. A white face often gets things done where a brown Filipino face may have difficulties. Courtesies and attentions may be paid which have no relationship to the actual status of the individual. Although polite behavior is traceable to a strong Filipino sense of hospitality and courtesy, white visitors may suspect that their light-complexioned skin is the primary factor in many of the considerations shown to them. The terms "Sir" and "Ma'am" are used frequently when referring to foreigners, even in constructions such as "I gave the book to Sir." An American also tends to be seen as an "expert," whatever the actual case may be, and this too can have a negative impact on communication across cultures.

Travelers to the Philippines do well to remember that Filipino society is very much in transition, in search of its underlying identity. While the effects of a colonial past are still visible and instrumental in day-to-day interaction, many Filipinos are consciously freeing themselves from old patterns of behavior and thought. The colonial past is being critically examined with an eye toward understanding the subtlety of its effects, desirable or not. Even though anti-Americanism exists in the Philippines, there is also a widespread feeling among both Americans and Filipinos of an enduring linkage between the two countries, almost a feeling of family—a specialness that shows promise for a true and lasting friendship someday. As nations, that may be some time in coming. As individuals, it is realized a hundred times a day.

3

The Essential Filipino

The literal meaning of the expression *kinaiya* in the Visayan language of Cebuano can be translated as "the way it is." Appropriately enough, it conveys the concept of customs, as well as the idea of "suchness" in referring to the peculiarities in someone's character. Maria is difficult to deal with because that is her kinaiya—the way she is. Filipinos do this or that because it is their kinaiya—their custom, the way it is. Embodied in this expression is an acceptance of their beliefs, values, and social behaviors as givens, a view which Filipinos share universally with other cultures. Just as people in general do what they do without being very aware of why, Filipinos see their behavior as the way it is. They hold certain beliefs or adhere to certain values without being concerned about how these beliefs or values came to seem correct and normal.

Americans are no different in this respect. While the term "un-American" often has a political or ideological usage, for some it also conveys a broader sense of "not-rightness," identifying a behavior or point of view as one outside the accepted norm. Even diet has norms. The fact that hamburgers are the universal short-order food in the U.S. seems perfectly normal to Americans. They would be surprised to go somewhere and find it otherwise. Similarly, family mobility, do-it-yourself home repair, personal choice in matters of religion and marriage, "plain speaking," the belief that all problems are inherently solvable, and many other aspects of American society have a similar suchness about them. Sociologists may study and quantify such expressions of the American culture, but for the average person it is the way things are and therefore appropriate and correct.

Our attention in this chapter will be on some of the essential values and beliefs which make Filipinos what they are. In some respects we find a clear contrast with American values and beliefs. In other respects, the difference is more one of emphasis. Filipinos and Americans may hold quite similar ideas about basic, underlying values and purposes yet express them in quite different ways in their personal behavior. The idea that people are all essentially the same may be a valid spiritual concept, but in communicating across cultures it can lead to simplistic perceptions and serious problems.

Individualism

An American wanting to understand Filipinos does well to start by remembering how important it is in the United States to be an individual—and all that implies. From earliest childhood, American values virtually begin and end with an emphasis on the self. The American political system was founded on a belief that people will pursue their own self-interest in their personal lives and that the aggregate effect of these pursuits, properly regulated, will culminate in the common good. To protect the right of people to pursue their own self-interest, checks and balances and other safeguards are built into law and the Constitution. American children are told to think for themselves. They are expected to make decisions about careers, friends, marriage, where and how they live, and even about their personal faith. As long as no laws are broken or other people injured, Americans believe they have the right to do pretty much as they please. If family or friends approve, then so much the better. If they do not, self-respect and being true to oneself demand that one's personal star be followed anyway.

The fact that a great deal of conformity exists in American society is not cause to discard the ideal. It is the *value* which is important. The sanctity of the individual is an underlying and enduring attitude among people living in the U.S., and it deeply influences their patterns of thought and action. Where would half of our literature and most of our popular entertainment be without the theme of the individual struggling against odds toward some self-defined goal?

Because all this seems so natural and preferable to most Americans, it may be difficult to believe that there are those who think differently. Yet individualism and its expression in the United States may be the most profound value gap separating Americans from much of the rest of the world—including the people of the Philippines. Americans interact in ways which follow logically from the centrality of the individual: with directness, informality, and belief in the virtue of frankness and sincerity ("Tell it like it is"). Americans are impatient with detours or indirectness ("Let's get to the point") and disdainful of rote learning, with the corresponding belief that the ultimate authority or test of truth is one's own ideas and conscience. They place a high value on objectivity, innovation, and practicality. These attributes form a paradigm for what Edward T. Hall has defined as a *low-context* culture: a culture in which social institutions, structures, and systems (the context) are given less emphasis than the individual person.

By contrast, the Filipino lives in a *high-context* culture. From early childhood, Filipinos learn the importance of the groups or contexts in which they live—family, neighbors, the *barkada** (peers), associates at work, and other, larger loyalties and identifications. Filipinos consider themselves individuals, but within a group. They are defined by, and linked to, the identity of the groups of which they are members. The Filipino way is to acknowledge the fact that human beings live within vital circles of associations, whether they like it or not. These identifying circles offer a field of action, support, and meaning even as they help define the persons within them. Thus, it is important to be connected with many circles. To achieve this requires that Filipinos concern themselves

* See appendix 2 for a listing of common Filipino terms.

with all that affects a person's good name and prestige, such as sensitivity to the moods and quirks of others and the development of skill in handling interpersonal situations. Consequently, it is important to be loyal and supportive of the family, friends, and associates who sustain the person throughout the vicissitudes of life. As a result, the Filipino demonstrates a highly developed sensitivity to what, in behavioral terms, would be called *interactive process*. Observing how people sit or hold their arms and what signs of stress, anger, friendliness, or ease they exhibit is as important (or more so) to the Filipino as listening to the words being spoken. Tone of voice—preferably soft and polite—is vital to Filipinos. Maintaining good relations with other people is more significant than being "right" or getting a particular task accomplished.

Sensitivity to others is matched by an equal sensitivity to how one presents one's self. Filipinos often search for clues about how they are being seen by others: Is that a put-down remark? Is she being sincere? Has that caused my family to lose face? What will "they" say? How many of those invited came to the party? How will it look if my friend does that? Among Americans, sensitivity about one's self is also normal and expected, but it is usually on a personal level, without the Filipino tendency to feel implicated in any adverse commentary about one's friends, family, and associates. The idea that a family might be discredited for the actions of one of its members seems totally unfair to Americans while in the Philippines it would seem quite appropriate.

It would be difficult to overemphasize the importance of this difference between the Filipino and American cultures. A great number of secondary values and behaviors on both sides stem from a fundamentally different perspective on the rights, roles, and obligations of the individual vis-à-vis the circles of relationships he or she maintains within the social framework. In no way does the Filipino approach imply a lack of regard for the individual person. Similarly, American individualism does not deny the larger society. To be an American, however, normally means to be reared in an atmosphere emphasizing and reinforcing one's personal autonomy. Behavior is a *personal* matter—one which does not necessarily imply that others need to concur. "Live and let live," "Do your own thing"—these are the watchwords of American culture.

This basic difference in perception is central in several important Filipino values and traits related to

1. the role of the family,
2. relationship to authority, and
3. harmony in relationships.

These values might best be defined as "personal" although they have an effect at both individual and institutional levels. In addition, Filipinos profess a number of societal values embodied in such concepts as democracy, nationalism, and egalitarianism and in a general body of Judeo-Christian ethics. At times, personal and social values may be in conflict. For example, the ideals of the democratic process may run counter to the obligations a person feels toward family. Similarly, the idea of nationalism may be difficult to realize in the face of deep-seated identifications with a particular region, linguistic group, or other association. Generally speaking, the values people consider fundamental to their personal identity will predominate over social ones.

The Family

For Filipinos the initial group, and the one which remains central throughout life, is the family. Few Americans maintain the close contact, loyalty, and mutual support which Filipinos take for granted within their families. The family is the ultimate place of security, and a consideration of the needs of the family, often over one's own wishes and interests, is a serious obligation. As the Filipino matures, the family group remains bedrock and serves as a model for the development of other friendships and associations. Most of the same elements (strong loyalties, mutual support, and a keen sensitivity to the nuances of day-to-day relationships) carry over into these expanding circles, providing the context in which the Filipino lives and works.

This kind of family orientation is not typical of Americans. Although families often do maintain lifelong closeness, the form of the family relationship provides still another demonstration of the essentially individualistic nature of American life. Living apart from one's parents often starts after graduation from high school, and contact between family members can be limited to gatherings on holidays, telephone calls, and an exchange of Christmas gifts. If an American's relationship with his or her family is closer or further apart than this, it is a personal matter—not subject to the comment or expectations of others.

The Filipino family is not just an initial training ground for learning how to function in the world; it is a permanent, vital element in the entire life of the person. To a degree unusual in the United States, Filipino families are closely intertwined in each other's comings and goings, failures, and triumphs. To understand Filipinos is to accept the complete centrality of the family—and that means the extended family, including several generations. No other single aspect of life is likely to be as important, lasting, or influential on choices and decisions from childhood to old age.

Among Filipinos, the person exists first and foremost as a member of a family and ultimately looks to that family as the only reliable protection against the uncertainties of life. Children may remain at home for years after becoming adults. An elderly grandfather or retired aunt can expect to be taken care of in the home of a relative, not in a public institution or in the "Golden Age Retirement Center." A city family may have one or more "country cousins" living in their home—in a mixed role of domestic helper and family member. Maria and Jaime may have been sent to the urban relatives in order to prepare for a paying job, or they may be university students whose city relatives not only provide room and board but perhaps tuition money as well. They are distant cousins but still "family," and there is an obligation to help them if at all possible.

Going to college, taking a job overseas, and getting married may sometimes be individual decisions, but quite often they are family decisions. It is not uncommon to meet Filipinos who wanted to pursue certain educational or career goals but could not because an older sister had claim on the limited family resources, or a brother's job had higher priority. Jealousies and resentments are not uncommon, but the compensations are well defined: each member belongs, and each expects to have the family's love and support when it is truly needed. The Filipino relationship to family is not, however, just a practical trade-off of autonomy for social security. It is an expression of a fundamentally different way of perceiving the place of the individual in the social context.

Considerable sharing of material things—of clothes and belongings—is taken for granted. A Filipina can walk into a store to buy herself a blouse and come out with one for her sister instead. The sister, meanwhile, may be going through her wardrobe and deciding on several items (she still wears but can do without) to send to a cousin starting off on a new job in the next province. Sharing bedrooms or sharing the bed itself is commonplace between two sisters or two brothers. Sharing time together with family members and friends—not being alone very often—is taken for granted.

Other aspects of Filipino culture also reflect values rooted in the family. There is an almost automatic deference of younger to older, both within the family and in day-to-day interaction in school, social life, and work. Age is not a curse in the Philippines, and the older foreigner may pleasantly note that his or her age seems to warrant greater courtesy than that normally offered back home. A protectiveness toward females is pervasive in the Philippines, extending to an active preoccupation over matters of chastity and safety. Despite the emergence of Filipino women into the work force in recent decades, the rightful role of women is still strongly believed to be that of homemakers and mothers. Divorce is illegal in the Philippines. It exists, however, in several informal ways, most usually through a de facto separation. A mistress on the side, even another child or two outside the marriage are common enough to be recognized as basic facts of contemporary life. Yet, society tends to hold the marriage vows sacred; whatever a man's extramarital habits might be, he is expected to support his family and not humiliate them through abandonment or by flaunting his behavior. The woman is expected to be loyal to her marriage and to strive to maintain it. This is not always realized in practice, of course, though her infidelities are treated by society with much less tolerance than those of her husband.

Authority

In a society where awareness of context is emphasized, people are likely to have a strong sensitivity to matters of authority. Such is the case in the Philippines. The different ways in which Filipinos and Americans define and manage authority relationships illustrate one of the important cultural contrasts between the two peoples.

Authority in the U.S. tends to be abstract and impersonal, although for children it is quite personal. Even for American children, however, authority is often depersonalized in the form of rules, family policies, or perhaps the written advice of a child-rearing expert. As they mature, Americans encounter authority less and less personally—in the form of laws, regulations, professional procedures, union rules, insurance company decisions, and so forth. Most Americans, after becoming independent adults, encounter only two authorities face-to-face (usually with a degree of anxiety present): the boss and the police. For millions of Americans, dealing with these may be the main occasions when their sensitivity and expertise in interpersonal relations is really put to the test.

Among Filipinos, rules, laws, and other impersonal expressions of power exist. But to an extent not common in the U.S., Filipinos tend to see authority as something to be dealt with personally as best one can, which might mean subverting or defying it at times. More often, Filipinos try to placate authority, keep it at a distance, or use it to their advantage where possible.

Authority in a Filipino home gravitates toward age and usually toward the males. A younger child is expected to heed the guidance of older children, who in turn yield to the mother, an aunt, uncle, or the father. Maturity does not fundamentally change these relationships. In a particular household, the father may be the final arbiter and authority, but he may be on the receiving end of advice and direction from his older brother down the block, who tells him how to run his life, handle his job, or vote in the election. Authority is always presumed to be present. In the home it is the eldest; in religion it is the priest; in school it is the teacher; at work it is the properly designated supervisor or those senior in rank. Individual Filipinos seldom claim for themselves full and final authority on any matter.

Filipinos think for themselves as much as Americans do. The difference lies in the way the two cultures condition the process. Americans normally see themselves as having sufficient inherent authority to make their own personal decisions and judgments. They do so, and are able to do so, because of a perception that the social institutions and structures around them are predictable and reasonably fair in their operation. They are taught to see authority as benign or amenable to influence through the exercise of the right to vote, by appeal to a court of law, or to public opinion. Ultimately, when Americans take principled, individual stands based on personal conscience, they are conditioned to feel safe in doing so, without fear of catastrophic consequences.

The conditioning process in Filipino society does not emphasize the making of individual, personal decisions, although obviously at times they must be made. The preference is for decision making within the group or for solicitation of advice from someone senior. Filipinos sometimes feel the need to have confirmation of the decisions they make on their own. The cultural dynamics at work here depend largely, of course, on the degree of seriousness of the matter being decided. Filipinos and Americans are both likely to go about making crucial decisions in much the same way, getting advice and help in the process. The difference becomes clearer at the more ordinary, day-to-day level of decision making, where the Filipino tendency to enlist the opinions of others is much more pronounced than the American.

Filipino culture also tends to find the authority for action in group consensus. Identification with and loyalty to one's barkada is very important. At times, peer pressure and the expectations of one's friends result in behaviors which go beyond what the individual Filipino might do on his own. An example of this can be found in the degree to which many Filipino males display a macho image among their friends by consuming considerable beer and whisky, engaging in "one-night stands," hanging around the pool hall, and risking the family's income on gambling at the cockfights. One's barkada is not necessarily fixed for life, but at any one time Filipinos will feel themselves to be a part of a definable body of schoolmates, neighborhood friends, or colleagues at work. Essentially, the barkada is an identifying and supportive element in a person's life. The existence of peer groups among colleagues at work is an organizational fact of life. For example, if a Filipino employee presents a grievance or contests a decision made by management, he will probably do so only after he is sure that he has the agreement and encouragement of his barkada. Typically, such a grievance would be presented by a small group of three or four representatives of the larger body of staff concerned.

Authority also resides in established institutions within the society, such as, for a great many Filipinos, the church. The authority of superiors is not normally a matter for debate for the simple reason that they have been appointed to their positions. Customs and the right of elder over younger are other examples in which authority is already established. The written word tends to have an inherent authority, and Filipinos are much more likely to be comfortable in discussing a troublesome matter face-to-face with a superior than in putting the subject into a memorandum. Not only does a written communication remove the possibility of seeing how one is coming across to the other person, but to Filipinos it also smacks of forwardness or presumption—implying "What I have to say is so authoritative it deserves to be written."

Filipinos are quite familiar with the reality of authority in their lives. For much of Philippine history, power resided outside themselves, in the form of colonial overseers and the institutions of control. Still influenced by that experience, Filipinos today are hardly surprised when authority and privilege are exercised arbitrarily. Where power is distanced by layers of abstract legality or by vast differences in social status, Filipinos historically have had (and still have) small reason to feel confident. The authority which can be most trusted is that which allows for some avenue of communication. Filipinos perceive authority to be ultimately *personal* and thus subject to influence and affiliation. The feeling underlying this perception is that whatever the law or the rules might say, somebody up there is making decisions based on personal motivations, worthy or not. Additionally, that person is potentially subject to influence—if not by me, then certainly by someone. How one deals with authority is therefore important and has implications for one's family and associates.

Harmony in Relationships

The interpersonal skills needed to deal with authority are essentially the same as those needed to manage a single relationship successfully. These skills, however applied in practice, are linked to a central core of fundamental cultural traits and values which create and define the Filipino character. At their most basic level of function and purpose, these values contribute to the creation and maintenance of secure and sustaining human relationships. The ultimate ideal is one of harmony—between individuals, among the members of a family, among the groups and divisions of society, and of all life in relationship with God.

Three of these values are of primary importance:

1. *Pakikisama* (getting along with others)
2. *Hiya* (propriety/shame/face)
3. *Utang na loob* (a consciousness of indebtedness)

These translations are all inadequate since the true meanings of the terms are complex and not always translatable. These values are deeply embedded in Filipino culture and influence behavior, whether an individual is conscious of it or not.

Pakikisama

Pakikisama represents both a value and, at the same time, a goal. "Getting along" is not something which just happens among Filipinos; it must be fostered. Filipinos who have been exposed to university courses on Philippine culture sometimes use the English acronym S.I.R. to refer to the concept of "smooth interpersonal relations." Achieving S.I.R., as noted previously, may often take precedence over getting a particular task accomplished. Filipinos are constantly aware of the need to be on good terms with those around them. Obviously, this is not always possible. As with any other people, Filipinos have their personal likes and dislikes, friction between personalities, and conflicting viewpoints and objectives. They differ from Americans in being less willing to let personal anger or friction become visible and are more uncomfortable when such tensions occur. Pakikisama is pursued by a variety of means: being conscious of it as a value and goal, showing sensitivity to hiya and utang na loob, being aware of and respectful toward authority and age, being thoughtful in how one speaks and acts, and by a host of other ways ranging from remembering birthdays to being responsive to indirect negotiation on potentially troublesome matters.

Hiya

Self-esteem among Filipinos depends to a significant degree on acceptance within one's circles of social and professional relationships. Hiya connotes a number of related ideas concerning how one appears in the eyes of others. Among these, perhaps face has the broadest and most useful application. *Face* is a term which can be heard quite frequently in statements like "She (or he) has a thick face," meaning that she flaunts shamelessness, or doesn't care what people say, or perhaps that he is pushy or self-assertive, lacking *delicadesa* or modesty. Fear of embarrassment, of losing face in a given situation, is strong. This fear is not just for the person alone but for the reflection on his or her group or family. A man might help out his nephew, whom he perhaps dislikes, only because the difficulties of the young man cause a loss of status for the whole family. A strong concern for face is a natural consequence in a society in which relationships (contexts) are central. For the Filipino, face and pride—and ferocity in defending them—are not light matters; they can lead to violence.

In the Philippines, pride takes on a significance which goes well beyond the American norm. The Filipino term, *amor-propio*, has a literal meaning of "self-respect," but that translation conveys little of the power and meaning the term has for Filipinos. Face and amor-propio are closely connected, but there is a major difference between them. Filipinos might withstand a loss of face in a particular situation, especially where they perceive themselves to be at fault. But to allow oneself to be insulted or belittled or to lose one's self-respect is intolerable.

It thus becomes important to behave in a way that insures that everyone's face and, particularly, everyone's amor-propio are not threatened. This translates into a Filipino characteristic which can be highly agreeable to the foreign visitor: an ability to get along with people, a tendency not to raise issues; and if a problem is posed, to offer a solution modestly as in "This is just a suggestion." Authority is treated respectfully, and the suggestion (which may have been formulated after long nights of private anguish) can readily be withdrawn at the slightest hint of discord. The request that deserves a definite no will, instead, receive an answer that sounds almost like agreement. Americans, therefore, can also find this aspect of Filipino culture exasperating. It goes against the frankness and directness—and by extension, the honesty and sincerity—which Americans judge to be right.

Utang na loob

Maintaining relationships requires the balancing of obligations and debts. A consciousness of obligations and the giving and receiving of tangible and intangible favors are highly characteristic of Filipino society. Americans also repay favors and debts but not with the Filipino's degree of concern for keeping the scale of obligation in balance. In the U.S., the discharge of a personal obligation has a liberating function, releasing the individual to go on being him- or herself. Among Filipinos, utang na loob serves an opposite function: it binds the persons involved more closely.

Utang na loob permeates all aspects of the culture, affecting broad political and commercial processes as well as the intimate relationship between siblings. It influences the decision on which families are invited to a daughter's wedding, the price paid for a gift, the number of votes for a candidate, and the processes used in finding employment. For example, how can Carmen get a job? To have her stand in the employment line is certainly not desirable. The best way is through personal contact by an intermediary (Uncle Ramon) who, because of past favors or other connections, can reasonably expect a warm reception by the company president (Mr. Roxas). The legal services Uncle Ramon provided to Mr. Roxas last year can be used to advantage. Mr. Roxas won't refuse to see Uncle Ramon, and while they are talking, he can just mention ... as a suggestion, perhaps ... that he has a niece who would make a good addition to the firm. One thing balances another. Uncle Ramon will take the assignment because he is sure that Mr. Roxas will treat him with respect and not cause him to lose face with a flat rejection.

Reciprocity also appears in the relationship between those in authority and those subject to it. The boss in a firm is more than just the person in charge. He (more seldom, she) is expected to know his employees and to be concerned about their welfare, to take the time to chat about a son's progress in school or a grandmother's death. This paterfamilias role is not specifically defined as such, and some modern Filipino management training, derived from American training practices, ignores it completely. But the traditional Filipino expectation is that authority figures have an obligation to be responsive. They can be approached, cajoled, influenced, and persuaded to provide what the person desires. The accent is on the personal, with the overall objective (for both the authority figure and subordinates) of maintaining a harmonious group relationship.

Some Other Filipino Cultural Traits

In addition to the values discussed above, there are also other aspects of Filipino culture that deserve attention, and they will be discussed in this section.

One of these values is a respect for tradition. While any visitor to Manila can easily see how much Filipinos like what is new, from movies to computers, not so visible are the traditional views and practices which Filipinos hold dear. For example, All Souls Day is not just a date on the calendar; it is a time for gathering at the family burial sites—even for camping out there all night—to pay respects to those who have gone before. The Americans brought Valentine's Day to the islands; yet nowhere in the U.S. will one find such devotion to hearts and flowers and greeting cards as in the Philippines. From weddings in white to gift giving, from caution about tree spirits to observance of holidays, Filipinos hold to tradition with as much naturalness as they buy the latest hit rock record.

In both the American and Filipino cultures, high value is placed on hard work. The difference is that Filipinos admire mental work far more than physical. Mainstream Americans are more comfortable with people who work with their hands than with those who work with their heads. A candidate for public office wins votes (so the saying goes) by demonstrating the common touch—by being photographed chopping wood, whipping up a cake, or talking to the gang on the factory line—not by writing a treatise on politics. Corresponding to this egalitarian ethic, Americans tend to see carefulness in diction or language to be an affectation. Education and intellect are not always reflected by an American's dress or manner of speaking as they usually are by the Filipino's.

Filipinos are widely regarded as excellent workers, and they perform well whether their job involves physical tasks or highly sophisticated technical functions. They are also strongly home- and family-oriented. Despite this, the low wage levels in the Philippines and the scarcity of good employment cause large numbers of Filipinos to uproot themselves to work abroad. The opportunity to earn dollars or other hard currency constitutes a motivation powerful enough to endure pangs of separation and the culture shock of living in a foreign land. A Filipino working in the Persian Gulf region (generally lumped under the inaccurate term "Saudi") may earn a thousand dollars a month—and send almost all of it back home to help the family. Overseas employers see Filipinos as assets because of their familiarity with English and their academic and technical training. The sheer need among Filipinos for decent employment, however, makes them easy prey to unscrupulous operators, foreign and Filipino, who entice men and women into situations amounting to a form of bondage. This can be particularly perilous for Filipino women. Numerous stories circulate about Filipinas who travel to Japan or the Middle East as household domestics only to end up as enslaved concubines. The large numbers of spouses and families separated for long periods because of overseas employment has given rise to a separate branch of sociology to study the phenomenon.

Status constitutes a potential source of discord between Filipinos and Americans. American egalitarianism tends toward underplaying differences in status—even if, and maybe especially if, the persons concerned are quite aware of them. Not so in the Philippines. While camaraderie and a softening of status lines exist among Filipinos, observances of respect are more common and more expected than in the United States. For example, it is "Engineer Ramos," not "Mr. Ramos" (who happens to have an engineering degree). In Filipino eyes, Americans have status, almost automatically. Accordingly, Filipinos expect Americans to have the appearance of respectability, which on one level may mean simply being well groomed, properly dressed, and carrying oneself with an air of self-possession. On another, it may mean acting and speaking in the way a Filipino expects of an educated person. These expectations may bother Americans, who do not like to be judged by what they believe to be superficial criteria. Most Americans prefer to be defined by who they are and what they have accomplished, rather than by the accoutrements of wealth or education.

A status marker which causes most Americans considerable discomfort is skin coloration. As noted earlier, Spanish and American colonialism taught Filipinos to be very conscious of the color of their skins:

"Which Maria? I don't remember her."

"Sure you do. She's fair (or dark) ... from Cavite."

The two descriptors, skin color and origin, may well come before any others, such as "She's the one who used to work in the art department."

The consciousness of small gradations in hue can be surprising to many Caucasians to whom Filipinos in general probably appear rather light-complexioned, or at least rarely dark. In English, Filipinos refer to themselves as "brown" when comparing themselves to Europeans or Americans, who are "white," even if the actual shade of color of many Caucasians may be darker than that of the "brown" Filipino. For centuries of colonial rule, "white" meant everything associated with the ruling classes: worth, beauty, desirability, and power itself. The lighter-skinned Filipino usually has either Chinese or Spanish blood in the family line. It is interesting, therefore, that being Chinese is not, in itself, necessarily desirable. A degree of antipathy exists among some Filipinos toward the more clearly Chinese among them, particularly those who cling to the Chinese language and cultural practices. An economic element seems to be at work in this attitude—a feeling that the Chinese Filipinos are too aggressive, or too much in control of money and business. Having Spanish ancestors somewhere in the bloodline, however, is likely to be a point of pride.

Lighter faces generally appear in advertising and on television. The more Caucasian a model looks, the better. Filipinas sometimes compare their own faces unfavorably to those of European or American women, deeming a flat nose, dark or brown complexion, and straight hair to be undesirable. Filipino young men and women may be pressured by their families to find lighter-complexioned mates. Acquiring a deep tan at the beach has never been a social goal.

Commenting upon a person's skin color is not as acceptable today in the U.S. as it once may have been. Sensitized to issues of race or ethnic origin, the American tends to shy away from direct reference to color, at least in polite conversation. Americans engaging with Filipinos may find it difficult to see much difference in hue between one Filipino and another and to use such differences in describing a person, as Filipinos consistently do.

Education also boosts one's status significantly and is a means of raising the entire family's circumstances. As such, it is worth sacrifice and effort. Students are expected to study, although the rigors of learning may vary considerably between one school and another. When one has reached a point of some accomplishment, it is not something to be passed over lightly. The neighbors share the news; the local paper may carry the story; mention is made in letters to relatives abroad. Correspondingly, if one is well educated, then, as we said above, Filipinos expect that person to talk, act, and dress the part.

Education beyond the elementary level has a special significance for Filipino women. In a largely rural and agricultural society, where employment opportunities are even more limited for women than they are for men, a bachelor's or master's degree can be the only alternative to marrying the boy from the *barangay* (village or neighborhood) and repeating the cycle of home, children, and village. Finding a marriage partner may not be easy, however, given male attitudes not uncommon elsewhere: by the time she is educated, a woman may be deemed too old to marry. She probably thinks so, herself, if she's more than twenty-five. If that is not enough of a problem, then her education may be too daunting to the men she meets. Despite such discouragements, however, women actively pursue education. Not surprisingly, the woman's endeavor is not for herself alone; it is a means of benefiting her family. Everyone gains luster when Maria gets her degree. Quite likely, everyone chipped in to help pay her expenses. Her salary and her pay increase when she gets a promotion will not likely all go to her. The more she makes, the more relatives there are needing her help.

Several traits found liberally among Filipinos cluster around values which have strongly religious overtones. Patience, endurance, and fortitude are among them, as is loyalty. To some extent these traits may be associated with women more than with men. In any case, Filipinos tend to admire the person capable of bearing a burden gracefully. A streak of fatalism is apparent here, expressed sometimes in the saying, *"Bahala na"* ("It's up to God," or "Leave it to God"). It is quite possible to work closely with Filipinos and not realize, for example, that the secretary who smiles so cheerfully has a sick mother miles away whom she cannot visit because of the expense. The section chief, who goes about his work quietly and pleasantly, may have a private grief known perhaps only to his closest associates. Outwardly, virtues such as fortitude and forbearance, in concert with other cultural traits, contribute to the maintenance of the social harmony which Filipinos seek. Filipinos do not bring their troubles to an occasion where they are inappropriate; they absent themselves instead. To do otherwise would cause the Filipino to appear insensitive or so egotistical as to believe that his or her private concerns outweigh those of the group. While Americans are also hesitant to impose their troubles on others in this way, they are more likely to wear their problems and emotions on their sleeves and let them intrude into their social activities.

Religion, particularly Roman Catholicism, has played a major role in forming mainstream Filipino culture. Certainly in outward signs—festivals, church-related customs, etc.—religious background is readily apparent. Below that surface, things are not so straightforward. On the one hand, virtues can be admired and, on the other, actual behavior can be quite at variance with recognized norms. The Filipino was first referred to as "split-level" by psychologist Jaime Bulatao, S.J.: making all the right noises to the priest about the evils of gambling, for example, and then going off to the cockfight to lose his week's wages. A tension has always existed between the overlay of foreign culture and values and those indigenous to the islands. Another split-level view of Filipino culture—less true than catchy and mindful of two successive colonial eras—has led to the old saw: "The Filipino is a product of four centuries of the convent and two generations of Hollywood."

Even while embracing modern science and pragmatism, the Philippines is a land where paranormal phenomena are an accepted part of reality. It is not unusual for conversation in a social gathering to turn to ghosts, tree spirits, psychic healing, and similar topics. Educated and conventionally religious Filipinos may cross themselves to ward off a possible evil associated with a tree along their route—one that perhaps stands at the scene of a grisly car accident. (There are favorable and unfavorable spirits at large in nature. Some trees seem to collect one kind, and some the other.) A coincidence is not merely a congruence of events but a meaningful occurrence worthy of discussion. Dreams are also taken quite seriously—particularly those involving deceased persons. Many Filipinos, however, discount the notion of spirits and other paranormal phenomena—at least on the surface.

Family, harmonious relationships, status, and authority are themes of major importance in understanding Filipino culture. We will encounter them again in the chapters ahead as they come into play when Americans and Filipinos meet, socialize, or work together. Always, the fundamental difference to be managed in the process is the contrasting view each has of the individual's place in the scheme of things.

7,000 Islands and Other Diversities

The Filipino values discussed in the foregoing chapter are only approximations of an intricate and diverse reality. Similarly, there are wide divergencies among Filipinos in economic status, outlook on life, political orientation, language, ethnic background, and a host of other elements which go together to make up the richness of Filipino society. Visitors would logically expect to find significant differences in attitude and behavior between an illiterate fisherman in Bohol and a filmmaker in Manila. Equally divergent will be the concerns and opinions of Filipinos struggling to make mortgage payments at the prevailing low wage levels in the country from those who go to Hong Kong to do their shopping. Many statements made about Filipino culture refer to the Christian areas in the north, where the majority of Filipinos live and which have little in common with the Muslim areas in the south. Visitors only meet particular people in specific situations. It is important, therefore, to place these encounters against the rich and diverse background of the country as a whole.

The Setting

The Republic of the Philippines stretches 1,150 miles (about the distance from New York City to Miami) from north to south and some 680 miles from east to west. The northern part of the country is closer to China (across the South China Sea) than many sections of the country are to Manila, the capital. It is a nation of islands—some 7,000 of them—ranging in size from more than 40,000 square miles to less than one. On these islands live 57,000,000 people, who speak more than eighty distinctly different tongues, eleven of which are spoken by enough people to qualify as major languages. The number of local variations and dialects are almost too many to count.

Three racial types are found indigenously in the Philippines: Negrito, Indonesian, and the predominant Malay. Add to these Chinese, Caucasian, and others in small numbers, and a perspective on the diversity of the country and its people begins to emerge. The Negritos may represent the earliest racial stock on the islands although their origins are mysterious. They are now relatively few in number, having long ago been assimilated to some degree or pushed aside by successive waves of Malay migration beginning well before A.D. 1000. Despite this mixed ethnic background among Filipinos, visiting Americans may see less variation in appearance than they are used to seeing in most major cities in the U.S. Filipinos, however, are keenly aware of the differences among themselves. Indeed, turning the tables on an old stereotype, they are likely to think that "all Americans look alike."

Religion

Christianity is the dominant faith in the Philippines, in particular, Roman Catholicism. During the centuries of Spanish colonialism, Catholicism was the only acceptable faith, and its teachings, vocabulary, and practices left an indelible stamp upon Filipino consciousness. For colonial Filipinos, unable to advance through political channels, membership in the clergy offered a significant avenue to influence and prestige. During the nineteenth century tensions arose between Filipino priests and Spanish friars, who were threatened by the growing importance of the indigenous clergy. The martyrdom of three Filipino priests in 1872 became one of the milestones in the development of an emerging national consciousness, leading eventually to the Philippine Revolution toward the close of the nineteenth century. American military forces arrived in Manila in 1898 as allies of the Filipinos against the Spanish, but they soon decided that "Manifest Destiny" demanded that the United States, itself, assume the mantle of Spanish colonial power. While the justification in the U.S. for this betrayal and seizure centered primarily on commercial and strategic gains, American Protestants were quick to see the Philippines as fruitful ground for missionary work as well. In a talk delivered at the Union Theological Seminary and entitled "The Christian Conquest of Asia," Reverend J. H. Barrows combined the two themes: "Wherever on pagan shores the voice of the American missionary and teacher is heard, there is fulfilled the manifest destiny of the Christian Republic...." President McKinley, a Methodist, asked, "Do we need their consent to perform a great act for humanity?"

Thus, American occupation brought Protestantism to the Philippines. Today, Filipinos exhibit a significant and growing interest in various evangelical and charismatic movements. *Iglesia ni Kristo*, an independent offshoot of the Catholic church, is widespread among the islands and is known for its strict moral rectitude and the regulation of its followers to the point of locking the doors on Sunday and taking attendance.

Islam was already a presence in the Philippines before the arrival of the Spanish and is still a significant minority religion today, predominant in much of the southern island of Mindanao. The historical tension between Christians and Muslims continues, and among Muslims a strong separatist movement spills over into direct confrontation and violence. And finally, a small number of pagan sects can be found in several regions, resistant to (or overlooked by) Christian and Muslim communities trying to win converts.

Regionalism

Regionalism is a significant factor in the lives of Filipinos. A person's place of birth, language or mother-dialect, and the common beliefs about that region play an important role in how that person is accepted by other Filipinos. For many, regionalism may not be an issue simply because they never move away from their place of birth, and they may rarely encounter Filipinos from other areas. In urban areas, however, or in a place of employment where staff may be drawn from a number of the islands, a person's regional identification will be significant.

The foreigner may be surprised at how often a regional label is attached when one Filipino discusses another. It is as if an American were to make a special point of knowing that "Joe comes from Montana, Mary was born in Alabama, Sue is an Oregonian, Tim a New Yorker." While this might be common knowledge among employees in an American office, the information would likely be only a point of interest, whereas in the Philippines regional labeling is not only much more pervasive but also assumes a high degree of importance.

The historical reasons for this stem from the fragmented character of settlement and development among the seven thousand islands. Only in recent decades has travel between various areas become commonplace. For example, Filipinos living in Ilocos Norte or Cagayan, at the northern end of the country, had limited contact over a period of centuries with people living on the other side of the mountains, much less with those at the southern end of Luzon; and the people in Mindanao might as well have been on another planet. Only under colonial rule were these scattered areas brought together as a single unit, which planted the seed of a potential national consciousness that slowly grew during the centuries of Spanish domination. Since the Philippines became first a commonwealth and then an independent country, a new sense of nationhood has been forged. Hindering this process, however, is the complex of languages, customs, and characteristics distinguishing the people of one region from another.

In managing a training operation in the Philippines which employed some seven hundred Filipinos from all parts of the country, the author confronted many occasions where regional sensitivity intruded. When a teacher was promoted to supervisor, for example, other Filipino staff might ignore qualifications entirely and seize upon the "explanation" that both the teacher in question and the chairperson of the selection committee happened to come from the same province. Filipino staff watched to see which provinces seemed to be more represented among senior positions. Dormitory preferences, when an opportunity to choose arose, tended toward regionalism. Superior/subordinate relations were sometimes influenced negatively by long-standing regional prejudices.

Language

Linguistically, all major Filipino languages are historically related. This does not mean, though, that a speaker of Cebuano understands someone talking in Ilocano. Whatever similarity various root words might have had at one time, centuries of isolation have produced distinct, and mutually unintelligible, languages.

Despite attempts during the Marcos regime to mandate Pilipino as the language of the Philippines, there is no true national language. Pilipino is primarily Tagalog, a language spoken by a minority of people in the region of Manila, with a handful of words invented or borrowed from other Filipino languages. Among Visayans living in the central group of islands, Tagalog (and by extension, Pilipino) is as much a foreign language as English—and less respected. Pilipino is, nonetheless, a required subject of study in the public schools throughout the islands. Educated Visayans and members of other language groups are quite capable of speaking and understanding Pilipino (which they call Tagalog), even if they usually disdain to do so.

Many foreign visitors are surprised to learn that Filipinos do not speak Spanish. In the area around the city of Zamboanga in Mindanao, a local language called Chabacano is heavily mixed with Spanish, but otherwise, Spanish today is decidedly peripheral. Filipinos know a fair number of Spanish words, mainly because these have entered into their particular regional language or dialect. English, however, is the foreign language of study and serves as the de facto national language in commerce, law, government, and often popular entertainment. It is the language of status, education, wealth, and authority.

Thus, American visitors and travelers come equipped with an attribute which has considerably more significance than it might seem at first. Characteristically, Americans treat their language casually; it is a means of communication. Most Americans would be surprised to think that they were speaking a "prestigious" language as they ask directions to the bank or demonstrate a pump mechanism to their colleagues. In the Philippines, however, the English-speaking American is voicing the language of distinction. In a Filipino family, for example, Chabacano, Cebuano, or Tagalog may be the normal everyday language—with a sprinkling of English words. Yet it is quite possible for the father, when admonishing a child, for instance, to summon up a tone of authority by employing a few English words, or even by shifting entirely into English if he can. Two educated Filipino friends normally converse in their local dialect, yet if the subject becomes technical, or especially serious, they may shift gradually into English. Some of the reason for the shift has to do with vocabulary—English is the language of modern psychology, business, science, etc.—but it is also related to the way Filipinos feel about the language. Things may be easier to say in English, or the use of English may serve to emphasize the importance of the topic. The speakers may feel that they can be more precise in English or that English is less personal and not as potentially threatening. However, the use of English can also be a sore point among Filipinos. If, in an ordinary transaction between two Filipinos, one of them addresses the other in English, it may be seen as an attempt to show off and to "put down" the other.

English in the Philippines is widespread, yet not as well understood as it may seem to be on the surface. The majority of Filipinos speak relatively little English. They may know quite a few English words, through exposure to English-language radio and television broadcasts or because a number of English words have entered into common usage in Filipino languages, but still find it difficult to say a full sentence. The Filipinos who speak English are the better educated, those who have lived and worked abroad, the providers of tourist services, or those employed in firms where English may be used as the lingua franca.

Despite the fact that millions of Filipinos cannot communicate well in English, American visitors to the islands are struck by how commonplace the language seems to be: signs in English are everywhere; English books are readily available; radio and television broadcasts are often in English; shopkeepers speak it, as do some people on the street. While this greatly facilitates contact and interaction between Americans and Filipinos, it can also be the cause of misunderstanding. English in the Philippines is not exactly American English. The two are close enough to make the language a functional medium of communication but different enough to sometimes be a problem.

English in the Philippines often contains an admixture of indigenous language elements—a word or a phrase used as the most economical expression of an idea. Patterns of intonation—the rhythm of sentences and the stress given to certain syllables—are also noticeably different. The particular intonation pattern of a Filipino's native language also has a detectable effect on the way English is spoken. For example, the sing-song quality of Ilongo may be apparent in the English spoken by someone from Iloilo. The phonological systems of the languages are also a factor. Because Tagalog distinguishes more vowel sounds than does Cebuano, a Filipino from Manila finds it naturally easier to make the distinction in English between, say, *bit* and *bet* than would someone from Cebu. Filipinos commonly have trouble with the sound of *f* since it does not occur in the indigenous languages of the islands. Thus, the word "Pilipino" is not only the name of the established national language, it is also the way most Filipinos pronounce the word *Filipino*. The American hearing the sentence, "I *prepered* this report," could easily be uncertain whether the speaker meant "I preferred this report" or "I prepared this report."

Adding to the tension surrounding the use of a foreign language is a Filipino tendency to equate facility in English with social class and intelligence. Since Filipinos appear to speak a lot of English, Americans usually presume their understanding of it is fairly comprehensive while often it is not. All this makes for potential strain in Filipino-American interaction, tension which the American is certain to feel much less than the Filipino.

The most useful approach Americans can take in this regard is to listen carefully and speak clearly. Highly idiomatic language is best avoided. "Bill had his nose out of joint because his boss was coming down on him" will not likely convey much meaning to the average Filipino. Americans who have tried to speak a foreign language should have no difficulty in appreciating the problem which some Filipinos encounter in conversing in English. Sometimes, simply replacing a specialized word with a more general one can mean the difference between being understood or not. Similarly, being alert to the fact that the phonetic stress in an English word may shift in Filipino usage helps comprehension. Indigenous Philippine languages regularly stress the next-to-last syllable. When this carries over into English, as in "What he said registered clearly with me," the American may need to have a second hearing. In sum, a willingness to speak a bit slower, pronounce more carefully, and listen for meaning are usually all that is needed.

Appendix 2 lists a number of English expressions which often have different meaning to Filipinos. The traveler may also find it useful to study the selection of Pilipino words and phrases which Filipinos may use when speaking English.

Other Diversities

Filipino cuisine varies from region to region, between town and country, and between economic and social classes. There is no one characteristic national diet, aside from a prevailing reliance upon rice, pork, and seafood. How these are prepared, however, will vary greatly from one area to another. A well-known restaurant in Manila specializes in "traditional" meals eaten off banana leaves with the fingers. Normally, though, Filipinos eat from plates with a fork and spoon (rarely a knife). The main meal comes at midday and might consist of dried fish, *adobo* (pork and/or chicken stew), rice, *viands* (anything eaten with rice, such as beans or other vegetables), sweets, and beer. Special occasions might call for *lechon*, a whole pig roasted on a spit over charcoal. Filipinos are just as likely, however, to enjoy hamburgers, french fries, pizza, pancakes, and Coca-Cola. French, Italian, American, Chinese, and Middle Eastern restaurants are found in large cities and are patronized by Filipinos and foreigners equally. Some non-Muslim Filipinos eat dog meat, but this tends to be looked down upon by educated people. A delicacy which may not go down well at all with an American visitor is called *balut*, an unborn chick still in the egg, feathers and all. Generally, Filipino food tends to be sweet or salty rather than bland or intensely spiced. Appropriate to a sugar-producing country, perhaps, is the degree of sweetness appearing in foods, often where the American would not expect it.

Filipino weather can generally be considered tropical or semi-tropical. Where a North American regards a temperature shift of over a hundred degrees in a year and thirty in a day as normal, the temperature range experienced by Filipinos might be hardly more than thirty or forty degrees Fahrenheit throughout a lifetime. Summer temperatures rarely go above ninety-five degrees, although the humidity can be oppressive, while during a cold December or January night, the temperature might be as low as sixty-five degrees. In the upper mountains, however, temperatures can be cooler, and the hills around Baguio, for example, have been known to have a touch of frost on a winter's morning. The prevailing warmth causes Filipinos to be especially sensitive to temperature changes. A sixty-five-degree January morning will bring Filipinos out in overcoats, scarves, and mittens. Most Americans cannot appreciate the "weather shock" experienced by many Filipinos traveling to the United States.

The Philippines is located geographically in Asia. Filipinos, however, aren't so sure they feel Asian. In recent decades, the Philippine government and some intellectuals have promoted the notion in an effort to create a stronger sense of nationhood and to distance the country from the effects of colonialism. Many Filipinos, however, question how deeply rooted they are in Asia. There is a general sense of being neither this nor that, of sharing something of the Pacific islands, of being heavily influenced by Spanish and American cultures, and of perceiving only a remote historical relationship with the major cultures of Asia. If asked what the people of the Philippines are, the Filipino answer may well be "We are ourselves."

In Each Other's Eyes

Tourists in the Philippines are exposed to a wide variety of scenes and settings but normally encounter only a narrow range of Filipino behavior. The short-term visitor is likely to go home with an impression that most Filipinos are polite, accommodating, uncomplicated, and friendly and that relating to them is relatively easy. On a limited scale these impressions could easily be completely accurate, depending upon the particular Filipinos a visitor might meet. Applied more generally, however, they would be misleading because they touch only the surface and arise from very limited contact with the true diversity of Philippine society and culture.

Americans and Filipinos who live in each other's countries over an extended period of time develop more sophisticated views. Interestingly, second impressions—American and Filipino—may proceed in opposite directions. Filipino tourists (and other visitors to the U.S.) often encounter some of the worst of American society: rude bus and taxi drivers, impatient clerks, violence on the street outside their hotels, passersby too much in a hurry to give directions or be helpful, and a number of other jolting and unpleasant experiences. They may go home saying "I'm glad I went, but..." If Filipino visitors stay longer among Americans, work or study with them, or meet Americans in their homes, they are likely to modify their first impressions with more positive perceptions and see the troubling aspects of Americans in a broader context. By contrast, Americans in the Philippines are likely to have positive, though simplistic, first impressions of Filipinos. After living and working with Filipinos for a while, their second impressions may be more critical. "The country is so beautiful, but I really don't like the way some Filipinos...."

It is useful for both Americans and Filipinos to know how they appear to each other once first impressions have faded. Such assessments, of course, are not shared by all Filipinos and Americans. Individual experiences are always essentially unique, no matter how commonplace the circumstances. Cultural contrasts are not the only factors at work. Personality differences and the details of a particular situation also help to shape the impressions two people from different countries have of each other.

Being an American in the Philippines

American visitors in the Philippines should start with an appreciation of the fact that to Filipinos they are not just any foreigners. Americans arrive as representatives, willing or not, of the most important country to Filipinos outside their own. Events in the U.S. are part of the daily fare offered by the media. Filipino education is heavily influenced by American teachers, texts, and concepts. Millions of Filipinos either know someone in the U.S. or hope to travel there themselves. American movies, products, tourist groups, and military bases are visibly in evidence. The American influence is often overpowering and may cause Filipinos at times to exhibit a sense of inadequacy vis-à-vis Americans. Americans may find their Filipino associates apologizing at the sight of a *nipa* hut, or for the traffic congestion they encounter, or for any number of problems and apparent deficiencies. Ironically, some Americans find these apologies quite appropriate. Because Americans tend to feel a little sorry for anyone not fortunate enough to be an American, it is a short leap from that attitude to one of taking Filipino apologies to be merely statements of regrettable fact.

Filipinos sometimes use the label "Third World" in depicting their own country. An incident involving the author in 1983 was both amusing and illustrative. While driving along one of Bataan's dusty back roads toward a fishing village with a car full of Filipinos, I heard numerous apologies about the condition of the road and references to the Third World. The main issue revolved around the fact that the road was not paved. When I remarked that I lived in Vermont, where unpaved roads are common, the Filipinos jumped to two conclusions. The first was that I was joking. When I insisted on the truth of the case, the Filipinos proceeded to the second conclusion. They began to congratulate me, apparently for my sensitivity at having dreamed up the unlikely story to make them feel better!

There is another side to this Filipino sense of inadequacy. Just under the surface they are very proud and sensitive to perceived slights—particularly from Americans. Filipinos *expect* Americans to feel superior and to tell others just how much better it is back in the States (which, of course, is exactly what Americans often do). But just as Americans become defensive when faced with criticism of their country, so do Filipinos. Few interactions can lead more quickly to hard feelings. The fact that Filipinos may disguise their resentment and even respond politely to criticism is no indication of the true feelings aroused by such unsolicited commentary.

Even when the American has not directly criticized an action as inferior, the Filipino may feel an implied slight. For example, in the Philippine Refugee Processing Center in Bataan, where hundreds of Filipinos work and live with a large American staff, an incident occurred over the matter of burning leaves. Filipinos burn trash and leaves for the same reason Americans do, with perhaps one additional objective: to smoke out pests and insects in their houses. A Filipina was busy burning a pile of leaves near a dormitory, assuming that if some of the smoke happened to waft through the building, so much the worse for the insect population. An American woman inside the dormitory objected to the smoke and went outside to complain. She felt not only assaulted by the smoke but irritated by what she assumed to be the Filipina's lack of consideration. Her angry protest was both forceful and self-right-eous. The results were a long and detailed letter from the Filipina to the camp commander and a summons by the camp commander to the American program director demanding that the American woman be off the premises within twenty-four hours.

The cause and resolution of this incident are revealing. The Filipina interpreted the American's protest as an "attack" on her dignity and amor-propio because it was delivered publicly and vigorously. This was bad enough in itself, but more importantly, the American woman's choice of issue—burning leaves—was interpreted as a slight on Filipino culture since it is a common Philippine practice. The Filipinos considered the objection to the smoke to be an example of "First-World" arrogance and an asser-tion of superiority (since the Americans would presumably not do something so mundane as burn leaves). The camp commander—ordinarily more pro-American than many Filipinos—felt that the honor of Filipino culture required the drastic step of dismissing the American woman from her job. When apprised by the program director of the fact that this particular American woman occupied a significant staff position, the camp commander's demand for her dismissal ceased immediately. Another element had entered in: the Filipino respect for status. The matter was resolved not by dismissing the offender but by requiring her to write an apology to the Filipina.

"What Bothers Me about Filipinos…"

If several Americans who work and live in the Philippines were asked individually what troubles them about Filipinos, they would likely produce a list with several items in common:

1. Filipinos take forever to get things done.
2. Filipinos can't deal with frank disagreement and open dis-cussion.
3. Filipinos react to decisions rather than participate in making them, even when invited to do so.

4. Filipinos won't come straight out with a problem—they get someone else to carry their message for them.
5. Filipinos ask too many personal questions.
6. Filipinos talk behind your back and gossip.

These complaints stem from the clash of one set of values—mainstream American—with the values and practices of Philippine culture. Why would an American find these Filipino traits annoying? In the sections below, we will examine each of these traits to throw some light on the sources of irritation.

Getting Things Done

American culture places a high value on results, on "getting the job done." Americans would like everyone participating in a meeting, for example, to understand the objectives of the group, to stick to an agenda designed to accomplish those objectives, to present his or her views energetically, and to come to a decision everyone accepts even if some may not be entirely happy with it. They normally regard the emotions which may be aroused during the meeting to be extraneous. Americans, characteristically utilitarian, expect everyone at a meeting to share a common urgency to achieve results in the least amount of time, regardless of personal feelings.

Filipinos attending such a meeting would tend to rank the maintenance of group harmony equal in importance to the accomplishment of its objectives. If an amicable decision can be reached during the meeting, fine. If, however, there are those present who are not comfortable with a decision which seems to be emerging, or with the tone of the proceedings, then Filipinos are inclined to minimize concerns about getting the job done in favor of making sure that no one leaves the room upset or offended. They prefer to let the matter rest for a while and hold another meeting at some other time.

Here, Americans are influenced by an essentially individualistic approach while among Filipinos a sensitivity to context predominates. The tendency of Americans to work impersonally and abstractly toward a goal contrasts with a Filipino concern for the affective aspects of a situation, an awareness of relationships which will continue long after the meeting is over. Americans see a democratic vote on an issue as proper and sufficient; Filipinos are more likely to prefer consensus.

Open Discussion

What happens when Americans and Filipinos are in the same meeting? Too often, the Americans end up dominating the proceedings, if only by sheer volume of words. Since such a meeting is almost certain to be in English, language fluency plays a part in determining what occurs. But, also, other important cultural factors come into play. The Americans expect each person present to be individually goal-oriented and to articulate his or her point of view—assertively, if need be. The Americans become engaged in the topic; speech quickens and becomes more forceful and sometimes louder. The Filipinos in turn become cautious, perhaps slide back a bit in their chairs, and, if the Americans persist, begin to look at their laps. The Americans see a stimulating debate or at least an exciting discussion and may think that the Filipinos are "opting out." The Filipinos, on the other hand, react to the tension they feel as voices become more urgent, which implies potential anger to them. The Filipino response may stem in part from the difficulty of keeping up with the rapid back-and-forth discussion going on in English, but a more fundamental cause of such withdrawal is embarrassment in the face of so much immodest self-assertion.

Participation in Decisions

"Everyone was invited to comment when the matter was under discussion. Now, you come saying you don't agree with the decision!" This could well be an American's response to a Filipino following the meeting described above. The Filipino concerned may have been quite uncomfortable with the decision, yet he remained silent, fearing perhaps that his ability to speak English was not sufficient to express his point of view diplomatically and convincingly. Afterwards, he brought his concern forward in a manner in which he was much more at ease—one-to-one. To the American, however, it seemed that the Filipino was trying to advance his personal view without the give-and-take of debate. It seemed that he was not "playing fair." Among Americans, being invited to express an opinion is a conversational courtesy. It is not required since everyone's right to express an opinion is taken for granted. In turn, the American expects that if people have had a fair chance to express themselves and there are no contrary views, everyone is either in favor of the measure or at least willing to comply with it.

Americans dealing with Filipinos, however, may be disappointed in this expectation. Filipinos are less likely to respond to an abstract invitation, that is, to see an implied or general call for opinions to mean that they are free to speak up. Issues of status, face, and personal modesty make this difficult to do. Filipinos are more comfortable with, and responsive to, a solicitation of opinion when it is couched in personal and direct terms. They expect those in authority to take into account the views of subordinates but to do so without a public request for them. If a particular Filipino's opinion is desired, then that person would expect to be asked individually to express it. His or her peers would know that this was not mere forwardness. Sending off a memo to the boss to tell him what one thinks smacks of having a "thick face," of presumption, of calling into question the authority of those in positions between one's own and that of the boss. It can also be a quick road to undesired personal attention from one's superiors.

Here, American concepts and values relating to authority—and personal autonomy—come into conflict with those held by Filipinos. Filipino society is hierarchical in spirit, American society egalitarian. In actual practice, neither is purely one or the other. Nevertheless, Americans encountering Filipino culture may be disgruntled with what appears to be two-faced behavior: apparently concurring in some matter—through failure to express (and defend) an alternative point of view—while being privately opposed to it.

Indirectness

Indirectness is a cultural trait that is particularly upsetting to Americans. "Tell it like it is!" and "Speak for yourself, John!" are only two of the many expressions common to Americans which convey a cultural disposition toward direct expression and a belief in what is considered objective information. Americans tend to be suspicious of people who do not "say what they mean." A touch of the covert, of the uncomfortably furtive, seems to be present in dealing with someone who speaks metaphorically, indirectly, or obscurely. Equally, it seems to Americans quite logical—and, indeed, obvious—that the person who has a concern or problem should be the one to state it.

The Filipino communication pattern in this regard contrasts significantly with the American. Cultural themes pertaining to authority, hierarchy, group loyalty and identity, personal pride, and face all enter in—with pride and face being perhaps the most important.

When there is a problem or an important request to be made, Filipinos will go to some lengths to avoid making the appeal directly. Instead, they prefer to introduce a go-between to cushion the transaction and escape the embarrassment that might result from presenting the matter face-to-face with the other person. An employee in a firm, for example, who feels that a deserved salary increase has been overlooked, may take the matter up directly if she feels reasonably certain of a positive outcome. If, however, she feels that her case is weak or that she is on unsure terms with her superiors, she will find an associate to present her case to the supervisor concerned. The go-between, of course, will not just march into the supervisor's office and state the problem but will approach the matter with some finesse, obliquely mentioning the injured party, perhaps touching on her monetary difficulties, and passing into and out of the subject in the midst of other topics.

Americans, who tend to ignore implications in a conversation—seeing it as a stream of topics to be taken at face value—may miss the point entirely. For example, if asked later what he talked about with the go-between (Ramon), the American (Roger) might recall something like this: "Oh, he came to discuss the office supply situation." If Roger even remembers those elements in the conversation not related to the purpose of Ramon's visit, he probably regards them as ordinary office chitchat and pleasantries. Meanwhile, the underpaid friend (Clara) is quizzing Ramon, "Did you see him? What was his reaction?" Ramon thinks he has made his friend's need perfectly clear to Roger. Clara then waits for a decision. Unfortunately, Roger does not even realize that something is supposed to happen. In such a transaction, it is hardly surprising that the entire Filipino staff—not just Clara—may jump to the conclusion that Roger is insensitive to the needs of his Filipino colleagues and subordinates.

Not all experiences with a go-between are oblique or difficult to figure out. The function of the go-between is to make peace between two estranged parties or to bring a request, problem, or proposal to the attention of whoever has the authority to decide the matter. It is often laid out quite explicitly—though the identity of the originator may be concealed—so that it is easy for the person in authority to respond. If his or her response is favorable, fine. If not, then the go-between can say, "It's only a suggestion, of course," and no one has lost face.

Americans living and working with Filipinos need to develop the ability to read cues and decipher subtle messages, starting with an ability to *listen*. Not only do problems with language lead to misunderstanding, but the nonverbal aspects of the exchange— the context in which it occurs and the communication style that is used—can also disturb human relations and intercultural communication.

Personal Questions

"How much did you pay for that suit?"
"How much do you make?"
"Are you married?"
"Where are you going?"

To Americans, these are either personal (and offensive) questions or inquiries which are permissible only if the appropriate context is first established. Unless, for example, the inquirer politely mentions something along the lines of: "Excuse me, I like your suit. I've been thinking of getting a new one soon and wonder how much something like that might cost," the individualistic American considers his privacy invaded. Curiously enough, the American penchant for safeguarding privacy can dissolve in a moment if the American thinks there is a *reason* for the question—witness the free and easy responses to highly personal questions on anything that looks like a questionnaire.

There are Filipinos who can be just as nosey and mindful of other people's business as Americans can be. But for the most part, when a Filipino asks these questions—whether of an American or anyone else—they are simply an expression of interest in the person. They are a way of showing concern or pleasure at seeing a person or of sharing in the other's condition or good fortune. They are a facet of getting along with others. That the questions are personal is the whole point. The actual content of the question may be only incidental. For example, Americans are often annoyed when encountering a Filipino associate who calls out, "Where are you going?" American culture places a value on forthrightness, and, instinctively, the American feels pressured to respond explicitly; for example, "Well, I'm going to the bathroom!" (if you must know). The question, however, is a direct translation of a common Filipino greeting, meaning in effect no more than "Hi." A quite appropriate answer, and one that Filipinos would likely give, might be "Just there," or "Just walking." (The American equivalent is the common "How are you?" "Fine, thanks" exchange.) The important thing is that a greeting—and a friendly response—has been ex-changed.

Gossip

The Filipino word for gossip is *tsismis*. It sometimes seems to resident Americans that Filipinos do nothing so much or so well as engage in tsismis. Since American culture views gossip negatively, despite widespread participation in it, tsismis is one of those elements on which criticism of Filipinos often centers.

Filipinos are not likely to defend their pursuit of tsismis, but American criticism on this point can lead to hard feelings since Filipinos do not necessarily regard tsismis as an unmitigated social evil. While personal malice and jealousy generate most of the gossiping which takes place, now and then tsismis may serve more positive purposes, acting as a sort of social leveler or a means of curbing those who presume to flaunt a sense of self-importance. Similarly, gossip may be the informational channel of choice when Filipinos wish to caution someone whose behavior offends the neighbors. Filipinos do not relish being gossiped about. "What will people say?" is a strong deterrent to actions which may bring down the censure of the *barrio* (village or neighborhood) upon the individual, the family, or the group. In a professional setting, gossiping also serves to relieve tension—as it does in an American office—and as a sort of litmus test. The amount of gossip and the nature of the statements being circulated reveal much about the common concerns and issues felt to be important by the work force. It is not unheard of for Filipinos to invent items of gossip aimed at passing a message of some kind to those in authority.

One difference between the two cultures concerns the sheer amount of gossip among Filipinos and the degree to which it centers upon male-female issues, which Americans are not likely to consider important. The question of who is sleeping with whom may rally American gossip into action, as it does Filipino tsismis, but Americans are not likely to be much inclined to care that

Georgia sleeps in the nude, that Maria and Ramon drove to Manila together, or that Jaime used to date Amor but was seen talking with Juliet. Nor will Americans immediately assume that since unmarried Susan has gained weight, she must be pregnant. Americans consider very little of their private behavior to be a matter for public concern. When they find their private actions or personal attitudes a subject of gossip, they feel offended to the point of outrage. Filipinos are equally hurt and offended by gossip but are more culturally conditioned to accept it as a social given.

"What Bothers Me about Americans..."

Just as Americans find certain Filipino traits troublesome, there are American behaviors which Filipinos find difficult. Our purpose in looking at both sets of impressions is to identify factors which interfere with good cross-cultural communication. If a number of Filipinos were asked to identify the things which bother them about Americans, their list would probably look something like this:

1. Americans are much too serious.
2. Americans don't mix with us.
3. Americans don't make good friends.
4. American dress and personal hygiene can be offensive.
5. Americans are insensitive.
6. Americans are cold and superior.

Just as Filipinos are not likely to criticize themselves for the traits Americans may dislike, Americans may be surprised to realize that characteristics which seem to them entirely appropriate and acceptable can be cause for distress among their Filipino associates.

Seriousness

To Filipinos, Americans often seem much too serious—too task oriented and lacking the light touch. The American tendency toward dealing objectively with the job at hand—and a corresponding impatience with factors (especially personal and emotional ones) which seem to get in the way—seems extreme to Filipinos. One example of how these approaches come into conflict is the different ways the two cultures define what is professional and what is social. Americans do their workplace socializing in small bits: a few moments at the water cooler, at lunch, going and coming from work, or on special occasions. Too much socializing leads to unfavorable notice. Filipinos, contrarily, create less of a dividing line between social activities and the business of a workplace. They may be busy but still see the task as part of a more important priority—maintaining smooth interpersonal relations and being a part of a larger whole. Filipinos are not inclined toward getting into a frenzy just because a job is there to do.

Life is to be enjoyed, if and when it can be. Filipino interaction contains much laughter and good-humored teasing. Like Americans, modern Filipinos succumb to the spoon-fed entertainment provided by television, movies, and radio. They are, however, much more used to providing their own entertainment than Americans are. Singing, parties, a "blow-out" (see appendix 2), just being together—all seem quite a necessary part of life. At a get-together, for example, people expect to be cajoled into playing a guitar, singing something, reciting a poem. Americans often find these occasions uncomfortable, particularly if they assume that their performance must be at some imagined level of excellence. Quite the contrary, what Filipinos look for is simply good spirit, a willingness to be a part of things, and a sense of fun.

Standing Apart

Filipinos are likely to feel pleased to have Americans present at a social event. It is the surest sign that the foreigner accepts the Philippines, wants to be with Filipinos, and enjoys their company. Importantly, it sets those Americans apart from the greater number encountered by Filipinos who are often criticized for their exclusivity. Americans in the Philippines generally find the company of their compatriots more appealing. Some of this is due, of course, to familiar strains and stresses of life in a foreign land and the corresponding need to be among one's own. Some of the reluctance is the result of timidity in associating with Filipinos and a fear that one may not be welcomed or may do something awkward or embarrassing. But while Filipinos are certainly capable of understanding these dynamics—and do the same thing when abroad—they tend to interpret American reticence as exclusivity. Given the particular potency of the American relationship, Filipinos are likely to see disdain or arrogance in an American's unsociableness rather than mere personal diffidence and shyness. Americans should be sensitive to these perceptions and try to accept invitations to Filipino occasions when asked, and to invite Filipinos to American parties and outings. Those who make the effort find they learn to enjoy themselves and feel much more a part of things. Socializing also strengthens the American's position at work as well as contributing to smooth interpersonal relationships.

Friendship

Americans can be very puzzling to Filipinos when it comes to their style of pursuing friendships and engaging in social relationships. They put a high value on being outgoing and may use the word *friend* to mean almost anyone from a colleague at work or the neighbor next door to someone with whom they have been close for many years. At the same time Americans tend to protect their privacy, reserving their deepest feelings and perhaps sharing information about the inner circumstances of their lives only with members of their immediate families, a close friend, or a professional counselor. Friendships are maintained, of course, but often with an unspoken agreement that what is shared is limited to certain topics, or that the relationship depends upon circumstances which may or may not remain the same. When asked, an American may say, "Sure, Celia is a friend of mine," meaning that she and Celia work together on the same church committee or live next door to one another and they like each other. If the relationship goes beyond mere acquaintanceship, she may say, "Celia is a close friend of mine" or "Celia is a good friend."

Among Filipinos, a sharper distinction is made between "friends" and "acquaintances," although in ordinary speech the difference is often blurred. The meaning of friend to a Filipino encompasses a far greater degree of intimacy and obligation than the usual American concept of the term. It would be difficult for a Filipino to consider life without one or more friends—meaning those with whom one shares life's joys and woes, one's aspirations, needs, problems, and triumphs. Such a person may or may not be from within the family; often not. Friendship is something which takes time to develop. It does not come about simply through social contact but through a process of commitment between the persons concerned. Implicit in friendship are complete trust and special caring, as well as the devotion of time to the well-being and situation of another. Filipinos expect their friends to lend them money when necessary, serve as go-betweens in delicate matters, offer moral support in times of trial, and counsel them in making difficult decisions. They feel, and expect to feel, a sense of loss when separated.

Close relationships are not unknown to Americans, but they usually don't involve the same degree of obligation and commitment. One of the reasons for the difference in perception of friendship is related to the American's mobility. Friends come and go as the American family moves from place to place, with perhaps a few relationships surviving the obstacles of distance, perhaps none. Another factor is related to the American's ability to compartmentalize relationships. American friendships often revolve around an activity or interest, such as a bowling friend, a church friend, or a work friend. Such friends often don't exceed the limits of the shared interest. In sum, the American may have no friends of the sort a Filipino would consider essential, even among those friendships the American considers to be close.

When a relationship between Jack, an American, and his Filipino associate, Ramon, has developed beyond casual acquaintance, a potential problem in mixed expectations may arise. If Jack thinks of Ramon as his "friend" and uses the term freely between them, the significance for each of them may be quite different. Quite possibly in Jack's mind, the fact that Ramon is his friend means "Ramon is a great guy. I really like him. It's fun to go places with him. He's made my stay here enjoyable." Equally possible, Ramon's idea of being friends means "Jack says we're friends, but he seems bored when I've tried to tell him about the problem with my grandfather's hospital bills. I wonder if he really likes me or is just saying so? I want to be really close with Jack and share with him what I feel as a person and what I want out of life."

If Ramon, counting on Jack's friendship in Filipino terms, asks for the loan of a thousand pesos to help meet his grandfather's medical bills, Jack may well be offended and feel put-upon. This is not how friends behave in the American terms he takes for granted. Such a request, as natural as it might seem to Ramon, will likely cause a strain to develop between the two men. Jack will suspect that Ramon has been merely using their friendship to get something from him. Ramon will think that he has done nothing more than what friendship implies and will be equally offended at Jack's refusal.

A similar misunderstanding can arise when geography has created a separation between Jack and Ramon. Perhaps the two of them have worked closely together for several years. Then Jack transfers home to the U.S., giving Ramon a parting hug with every assurance that they have been really good friends. Jack goes off, his mind filled with the upcoming readjustments back into American life. Ramon expects to hear from him soon, perhaps even a telephone call saying he has arrived. To Jack, Ramon is a part of an experience he has now left behind. To Ramon, Jack embodies an ongoing relationship. When all he gets from Jack is a Christmas card some months later, Ramon is deeply troubled and feels sure that in some way he may have offended Jack. It is difficult for him to imagine that Jack could look upon their friendship as merely a passing and pleasant relationship at a particular time and place in his life.

Personal Appearance

Americans may be surprised to learn that Filipinos sometimes find their choice of clothing and their personal hygiene objectionable. Appropriateness of dress, for example, is a matter of greater concern to Filipinos than it is to Americans. Values relating to status and authority are at the root of the Filipino's need to dress correctly. In the Philippines, a person of significance—and this by definition includes Americans—is expected to look, dress, and act the part. As humid and hot as the weather in the summer can be, status-conscious Filipinos still put on what they consider appropriate clothing. Women do not wear revealing outfits on the street or in the office, and the sight of a braless American woman with skintight jeans is an affront to propriety.

This does not mean that Filipinos are particularly formal in their attire in normal day-to-day activities, but they do tend to dress more conservatively. Women of all ages are more frequently seen in dresses than in slacks and blue jeans while shopping, visiting, or working. The most common clothing for women over much of the Philippines consists of a skirt and blouse, the latter sometimes worn loosely and not tucked in at the waist. Muslim Filipino women generally wear a *malong*—a long, colorful cloth which drapes from the shoulders to the ankle. In urban areas and particularly among educated women, clothing tends to follow Western styles and is readily available in department stores and shops. A substantial percentage of clothing worn by Americans in the U.S. is made in the Philippines. Filipinos, female and male, appreciate the same styles and materials they export abroad. This is particularly true for younger Filipinos, whose clothing is often indistinguishable from that which can be seen on any American street.

Filipino men also tend to dress informally for most activities. At one extreme, it is common to see Filipino men bare from the waist up, wearing perhaps no more than a pair of shorts and plastic or rubber shower thongs, called "slippers." This is not, however, how Filipinos with any pretensions to status appear in public. Western suits and ties can be seen in business offices, but the *barong* is more common. This is a long- or short-sleeved shirt worn outside the belt, over trousers. Expensive ones are made from white pineapple fiber and can be quite elegant. The long-sleeved barong, known as the *barong tagalog*, is considered to be completely adequate for any formal occasion, particularly if it is of good quality, with embroidery or other decoration. Short-sleeved barongs, sometimes known as "sports barongs," serve for any normal occasion other than the most formal. American men should bear in mind that shoes and socks are considered more appropriate than sandals, despite the heat and humidity.

Filipino men, as well as women, have a high regard for jewelry and wear more of it, and more often, than do most Americans. Gold is preferred to silver, and an antique ring or brooch, handed down through the generations or given as a gift, is more prized than something of modern design. Formal occasions always demand the wearing of several pieces of jewelry, the showier the quality the better.

In many offices, the question of suitable clothing is solved by having a company uniform. While Americans are accustomed to wearing uniforms in many work settings, they do not usually expect to find them in white-collar office situations. Among Filipinos, however, the provision of uniforms by their company solves two problems at once. The cost of personal clothing to the individual is reduced, and any potential competition among staff over matters of wardrobe is eliminated. No one need struggle to put together an outfit each day which will hold its own with that of others in the organization who may have a bit more to spend on clothing, or whose rank would otherwise be emphasized by the quality of what they wear.

Americans may be a little surprised to see Filipino toddlers dressed in reverse fashion to how small children are attired in the U.S. Until the age of about three, many Filipino girls and boys go about bare on the bottom and dressed on top, with no more on than a little tee shirt. This is mainly a matter of convenience, with the assumption that underpants at this stage of life would be soiled anyway. Infants, however, are completely protected against possible harmful airs, including having their heads covered with caps. After the toddler stage, clothing goes back on top and bottom, with shoes or bare feet, depending upon the status of the family concerned.

A not-so-rare Filipino complaint against Americans is that they do not bathe enough, which may surprise someone from the land of the pulsating shower. Filipinos are scrupulous about personal hygiene and have sensitive noses. The heat and humidity do not allow long stretches between baths, and some Americans tend to be negligent in this area. Another complaint, specifically directed toward women, concerns body hair. Filipinas shave their legs and underarms, and Filipinos find it objectionable when they encounter American and European women who do not.

Sensitivity

Filipinos are often disturbed by the failure of Americans to perceive the nuances of a situation. Americans tend to feel that it is important for them to "be themselves" and to adjust their behavior very little from one occasion to another. American culture does not place a high value on the hiding of one's feelings; rather, it values forthrightness. Filipino sensitivity to context, as indicated previously, extends from a keen awareness of appropriate speech and behavior in a given situation to a well-developed instinct for what is implied and not stated.

For example, if Maria fails to reply warmly to a greeting from Beth, she is sending a message. Beth immediately knows that something is troubling Maria and she begins privately to examine the possibility that she may have hurt Maria's feelings in some way. Maria considers that she has communicated everything necessary and would be embarrassed at being forced to put her injured feelings into words. A curt reply, silence where a response is expected, or the expression on the face is all that is needed. Beth will try to approach Maria later, indicating her concern and puzzlement. When Maria feels ready to talk about the problem, she will signal to Beth with a smile or by breaking the silence.

If, however, the other person were an American named Jackie, the exchange would likely proceed quite differently. When Jackie detects that Maria sounds subdued or curt in responding to her greeting, she simply approaches Maria directly and says, "What's the matter, Maria? Is something bothering you?" Maria is immediately reduced to embarrassment, acutely aware that other colleagues are listening, chagrined at being confronted with such a delicate personal issue, and angered that Jackie is so dense as to not comprehend the obvious.

Attitude

Of all the things about Americans which distress Filipinos, perhaps the most serious is something hard to define but which can best be described as attitude. Filipinos want Americans to take a genuine interest in them. They wish to feel that Americans respect and accept them as people, that they tolerate and accept Filipino ways, and—when working on a joint project—that they recognize the Filipino contribution to the project. Too often, Americans come across as cold or superior. They make the assumption that if any adjusting is to be done, the Filipinos are the ones who should do it, whether it be the choice of language, the procedures to get a job done, or the personal relationships that develop between them. Filipinos expect Americans to be frank and direct, but they are particularly sensitive to anything which smacks of criticism. In this context, tone of voice takes on particular significance. Americans tend to speak in louder voices than Filipinos do. When an American thinks he or she is merely talking in a normal voice while offering a comment on the work of a Filipino colleague, the Filipino may feel that criticism is being shouted for all to hear. Probably no other rule is as simple and yet effective for Americans dealing with Filipinos than to speak calmly, quietly, and sensitively. Where criticism is needed or comment offered, Filipinos pray that their American counterparts will do so gently and with tact.

Working Together

Americans in the Philippines may work with Filipinos as colleagues, as superiors, or as subordinates. An American business or organization will normally appoint Americans to the senior positions, but there may also be American employees in the enterprise who report to Filipino supervisors. Americans are also hired by Filipino firms and have Filipino bosses. In any of these situations where Filipinos and Americans work together on a daily basis, there are opportunities for cultural stress and miscommunication. Equally, there are opportunities to develop a deeper and more enjoyable degree of mutual understanding.

A useful means of examining the interaction between the two cultures is a case study. We have chosen a fictitious American named Tom, who has just arrived to take up his position as a supervisor of the accounting section of an imaginary organization employing both Filipinos and Americans. The staff of his section are all Filipinos. The vice president for finance, to whom Tom reports, is a Filipino, and the president is an American.

On being introduced to his new superior, Tom finds it difficult to hide his surprise and amusement when he learns that the given name of the vice president for finance is Boy. Within a few hours he discovers that Filipinos have several common given names which may strike Americans as odd. Amidst the Ramons, Marys, Vickis, Roberts, and Noels that he meets throughout the Filipino staff, Tom also comes across colleagues named Boy, Babes, and Bimbo. Filipino given names derive from Hispanic or American influences and are also drawn from indigenous Filipino sources. A few popular names sound more like nicknames to Americans than formal, given names. Filipinos may use them either way.

As he goes about the offices meeting people, Tom makes an effort to indicate his friendliness by shaking hands firmly. Like most Americans, Tom equates a firm handshake with sincerity and trustworthiness. He feels a bit nonplussed by the limp handshakes from Filipinos which he gets in return; the gesture seems perfunctory, perhaps even unfriendly, and he feels a little awkward because the Filipinos hold on so long. It also surprises him when many of the Filipino women he meets merely touch his hand briefly. At home in the U.S. Tom is used to women, as well as men, shaking hands firmly and briskly. Later he learns that it is not the custom among Filipinos to seize a person's hand in a powerful grip and pump it energetically. When a Filipina shakes hands with a man, she may just let their fingers touch to make it clear that there is no suggestive forwardness on the part of either.

During his second morning at work, Tom attends a meeting with his boss. Boy's secretary comes into the office and needs to pass between them in order to get a file. Instead of merely excusing herself and walking between them, the secretary assumes a kind of diving position. She puts her leading arm down and forward, the trailing arm up and back, ducks her head and upper body, then glides as unobtrusively as possible toward the pile of file folders. To Tom and to many Americans, this sort of behavior seems servile. To Filipinos it is simply good manners—a way of indicating an apology for disturbing the scene and a self-effacing attempt to say "Pay no attention; I'm not really here." Hardly any behavior could be more attention-getting, however, for most Americans.

Later that morning, Tom observes two Filipino colleagues passing each other in the corridor. As they approach, they simply raise their eyebrows in a little flick of greeting. He begins to see this behavior frequently among the staff and finds that Filipinos greet him at times in the same way. Like many Americans, Tom feels that something is lacking in the exchange. He is used to words being spoken, even if only a quick "Hi." After being at work a week, Tom observes that when his Filipino colleagues first meet each other during the day, they shake hands and exchange spoken greetings. Later in the day, it is enough to acknowledge each other with just an upward movement of the eyebrows. Nothing more need be said and nothing impolite or unfriendly has taken place. But failure to exchange this eyebrow-greeting or a little wave of the hand would constitute unfriendliness.

Communication goes on at a *paralingual* level in all cultures. Body language, context, facial expression, emphasis, and intonation all carry messages. Often this level of communication can be more important than the content of the words being spoken. Verbal and nonverbal messages coming from a speaker may even be contradictory, as when someone sitting tensely with a strained expression on the face insists, "I'm perfectly comfortable, thank you." Filipinos have a highly developed sensitivity to the nonverbal aspects of a situation. They are considerably less dependent upon spoken words than Americans are, and they sometimes weary of the flood of American speech they hear. For example, Filipinos might reply to the question "Where ...?" simply by pursing their lips and pointing with a lift of the chin in the direction intended. Nothing impolite is intended in the gesture, nor do Filipinos find anything to be lacking in the exchange.

Before long, Tom encounters some puzzling situations involving the word *yes*. On one occasion he explains something to a clerk and asks if she understands. She nods and says yes, but it is evident that she has missed the point he was making. On another occasion Tom asks a Filipino colleague if he can come to dinner that evening. The reply is yes, but the Filipino fails to appear as expected. At first, Tom assumes that the problem is one of English comprehension among the Filipinos. Later, he realizes that the Filipino yes and the American yes are not necessarily the same. Because Filipinos have a strong wish to be accommodating, they may find it impolite or embarrassing to say no. The clerk with whom Tom spent time trying to explain an accounting point felt that she would be showing a lack of appreciation for his efforts if she told him that he had failed to make her understand. The colleague Tom invited to dinner hoped that Tom would see that his yes was hesitant and understand that he had other plans. Eventually, Tom learns to translate the Filipino yes as "I think so," "God willing," "I'd like to but ...," "If that is what you want," and sometimes even as "Yes."

One of the things which bothers Tom about his Filipino subordinates is how often they seem to require explicit instructions when carrying out a task, rather than following their own judgment based on general principles. Sometimes subordinates bring questions to him about a transaction which is very similar in nature to one carried out an hour or so earlier. Tom decides that such situations are the result of insufficient training. When members of the section come to him with procedural questions, he takes the time to explain the particular accounting principles which apply in those circumstances. His subordinates listen carefully and indicate their understanding of the concepts he tries to get across. Unfailingly, they are appreciative of the time he takes to explain and teach. But Tom's training efforts seem to bring only partial results. One of his subordinates begins to exercise more personal judgment, taking the approach he has tried to impart, but the others, in varying degrees, continue to come to him with questions he feels are unnecessary. It irritates him that these subordinates apparently do not want to think for themselves.

As Tom's experience in the Philippines lengthens, he begins to see a connection between such patterns of behavior and Filipino cultural traits related to authority and face. Typical of societies that are hierarchical in spirit, Filipinos prefer being sure that they are doing the right thing, thereby avoiding as much as possible the risk of a loss of face which mistakes might bring. To value discovering the truth for oneself through trial and error or to take action based on general principles and expect things to work out appropriately are more American than they are Filipino. While it may not always be realized in actual practice, Americans prefer learning through personal discovery rather than through rote learning of facts from an authoritative and absolute source. In the changing society of the

Philippines, both approaches can be found. On balance, however, Filipinos tend to prefer explicit rules, delineated procedures, and clearly established authority. One result of this can be seen in the Filipino regard for regulations governing conduct in the workplace. Given the risks to face and harmoniousness inherent in person-to-person clashes, Filipinos feel more secure within a system of established rules and procedures than in one where decisions involving individual and regional biases might have free play.

Tom finds it quite agreeable to be working among Filipinos every day. The level of courtesy, the degree of friendliness, and the more relaxed pace are all improvements over what he has experienced in previous jobs in the U.S. Soon he feels that he is on good enough terms with the company staff to join in the frequent joking and banter which he hears around him. Sometimes his jokes make everyone laugh; sometimes, though, his jokes seem to fall flat or even have the unexpected effect of causing a Filipino to withdraw into uncomfortable silence. Puzzled, Tom begins to analyze these situations and discovers that when his jokes are about a general situation, or when they include laughter at himself, everyone enjoys them. But if he tries to joke about an individual Filipino or a particular problem, then his humor may not be appreciated.

Teasing, instead of tsismis, can be the Filipino method of choice when the goal is to modify someone's behavior or attitude. Thus, even when personal joking may be meant only in a spirit of fun by an American, the Filipino concerned may hear it as a form of criticism. As in other situations, language comprehension can cause misunderstanding. The point of a joke may depend upon a nuance of meaning in a word deriving from a particular American cultural context. Humor often does not translate well across cultural divisions, and irony is particularly risky. When irony can easily be perceived as sarcasm even within the American context, it becomes especially important for Americans to be careful when making ironical statements to Filipinos.

As he continues to work with the Filipinos in the finance section, Tom feels the need to understand how his role as supervisor is culturally perceived. He learns that Filipinos today are often familiar with American styles of management. This does not mean, however, that the cultural assumptions underlying American practice necessarily fit smoothly into the Filipino context. How the role of the boss is defined reflects a major difference in managerial styles. Does being a boss mean performing certain specific functions which begin and end within a well-defined and impersonal operational structure? Or does the job include being something of a head of a family as well? Filipino culture prefers the latter. The accent is on personal contact.

Tom gets an opportunity to learn from firsthand experience when the chief clerk in his section leaves the company and needs to be replaced. Tom announces the vacancy, hoping that one of the Filipinos in the section, Gloria, will apply for the position. Her work has been excellent, and Tom feels sure that she would quickly become a competent chief clerk. Recalling his American management training, Tom proceeds in what he considers to be a well-defined and proper procedure: an announcement of the job opening, individual filing of applications, screening and interviewing of candidates, and a final selection based, as much as possible, on objective criteria focused on skills and qualifications. This approach emphasizes equality of opportunity and the identification of merit through competition, both of which seem to Tom to be self-evident values.

Tom is puzzled when several people outside the firm apply for the vacant position but not Gloria or any of the other members of the section. Gloria's failure to apply is a particular disappointment since it seems to him that she must not be as highly motivated as he had thought. Why would she not display initiative and compete for the job? He interviews a number of applicants and decides to offer the position to Raul, a Filipino transferring from another company. There is no sign of displeasure among the four members of the section, but soon Tom begins to sense that the finance section does not function as efficiently and pleasantly as it did formerly.

Only later does Tom understand what happened. The four Filipinos in the section were waiting for an indication from him concerning his plans for filling the post. They were quite aware of who ranked highest in seniority among them—and who had the highest status. Status could be based on something as worthy as special talent and capacity, or it could be based on "connections"—a factor also of importance in the U.S., despite American ideals to the contrary. The four Filipinos expected that Tom would decide, in his wisdom, which one of them should get the promotion. If his decision honored seniority, so much the better. No one's dignity would be diminished if the most senior person had been advanced. If "connections" seemed to be at work in the decision, then the remaining colleagues had one thing to fall back on: they had not pushed themselves forward to compete for the job, which would risk a loss of face and the embarrassment of self-advertisement, with the underlying implication of thinking oneself to be better than one's associates.

The Filipinos assumed that their work, their contribution to the organization, and their seniority were quite well known to Tom—or should be—and that he would evaluate all factors properly in making the decision to replace the chief clerk. The four colleagues behaved in a manner heavily influenced by a culture which places high value on authority and face. It seemed strange to Tom that, in effect, Gloria and the others were waiting for his "permission": a nod, a hint, a formal or informal indication from him that this one or that should consider applying for the vacancy.

After digesting this experience awhile, Tom seeks some advice when it comes time to evaluate Apolonio, another of his Filipino subordinates. By now, he understands that such a process is loaded with cross-cultural booby traps buried in the history of American-Filipino relations—Apolonio's subordinate status, his apprehension about being found professionally lacking (also read "personally lacking"), and his nervousness about how Tom will proceed. Will Tom fault him on weak points and overlook his strong points or criticize him in a loud voice for all to hear? Can he expect Tom to be warm and friendly, or cold and impersonal?

This time, however, Tom tries to do all of the right things. He establishes a friendly atmosphere. He asks about Apolonio's family, showing a personal concern and interest in him. He adopts a nonthreatening, relaxed posture and uses a quiet, conversational tone of voice. After commending Apolonio on the way he is handling functions A, B, C, and D, he points out that E requires a little improvement. Apolonio acknowledges this, and they discuss the specifics of what is needed. The meeting concludes on a warm and personal note, with an exchange about their respective families. When Apolonio is gone, Tom sits quietly for a few minutes, evaluating his success at being cross-culturally sensitive—and hoping that Apolonio got the message.

Apolonio, for his part, leaves the room feeling quite satisfied with the interview. Back at his desk, he is joined by two friends who want to know how the session went. He tells them that it was a good meeting and that Tom is quite satisfied with his work. "There are a couple of problems with E, which we talked about, but I guess he's also not happy with the way I handle F since he didn't comment on it at all." Since Tom is now more sensitive to cross-cultural factors, he has accomplished exactly what he intended: a subtle, corrective indication to Apolonio that F also needs a bit of attention, even if it is not a significant enough problem at this point to be directly mentioned.

Bridging the Culture Gap

What is a personally autonomous, individualistic, frank American to do in the midst of *pakikisama*, smooth interpersonal relations, go-betweens, and *amor-propio*? How does a sensitive, group-oriented, soft-spoken Filipino deal with a straight-talking, self-assertive American? Perhaps it's a wonder that Filipinos and Americans get along at all.

Fortunately, they not only generally get along, they often like each other. The reasons are not all that difficult to find, starting with a sense of common humanity which helps to bridge cultural differences among people everywhere around the world. Like others, Filipinos and Americans are usually able to perceive something of the motives and dispositions of the persons they meet. Goodwill is not so difficult to recognize, even when circumstances may be troublesome. Most people are capable to some degree of seeing another person as a distinct and particular individual, even in the midst of an unfamiliar cultural setting. Cultural awareness and sensitivity are useful traits to develop, but they complement, rather than precede, a basic wish to understand and communicate.

"What We Like about You ..."

As we have noted before, Filipinos have a greater degree of understanding of American culture than people in most other countries do. American visitors to the Philippines encounter a prevailing sense of hospitality and goodwill among Filipinos, including a disposition to overlook or accommodate to awkward situations. Despite their greater degree of social formality, Filipinos are nevertheless relatively informal and relaxed—a trait Americans find agreeable and reassuring. Being able to relate on a personal level is the key, along with a healthy sense of humor. People who are able to laugh, particularly at themselves now and then, seldom have problems getting along with Filipinos.

A few years ago in an educational project employing both Filipinos and Americans, both groups were asked to name the traits of the other which they found agreeable. In effect, each nationality asked the other to "keep doing more of" the things which helped to bridge their cultural differences.

The Filipinos encouraged the Americans to

1. take an interest in Filipino culture and languages,
2. be friendly and "interested in us as individuals,"
3. recognize the Filipino contribution to what is going on,
4. continue to be frank and direct but also tactful and sensitive,
5. be professional in look, manner, and competence,
6. "bear with us" as nonnative speakers of English, and
7. make an effort to interact with Filipinos.

These make a useful "do" list for any visitor to the Philippines. Most of the items are not culturally specific; they are simply good manners or the kind of thoughtfulness which is valued in any society.

The Americans, for their part, appreciated the Filipinos for their

1. friendliness and courtesy,
2. cheerfulness when things go wrong,
3. willingness to be helpful and supportive,
4. concern for people as individuals,
5. use of English when Americans are around,
6. intelligence and willingness to work hard, and
7. familiarity with the U.S. and the American ways of doing things.

As one can see, the two lists are not parallel. This results from the fact that the Americans in the situation were the foreigners and also from some underlying differences in viewpoint. The Filipinos and Americans did not see each other from culturally equal perspectives. The Filipino responses offered guidance to the Americans about behaviors which were successful in Filipino cultural terms. At the same time, a note of appeal comes through. The Americans simply took the occasion to thank the Filipinos for the *Filipino* traits they found pleasant and appropriate. It is interesting that the Americans saw no need to help their Filipino colleagues relate to American behavior better but took for granted that Filipinos are familiar with things American. The two lists converge, however, in a mutual wish to be seen as individuals, not as representatives of their respective cultures.

Fellow Students and Teachers

It is in educational settings where Filipinos and Americans most readily enjoy a peer relationship, as students or faculty members. A number of well-known universities in the Philippines attract students from around the world. Institutions such as the University of the Philippines (hardly ever identified as anything but U.P.), Ateneo de Manila, and others are members of the American accrediting system of schools and colleges. Academic credit is transferable between these and many American institutions. American professors continue to play an important role in Filipino academic life as visiting or resident faculty and researchers.

A kind of unintentional, and not necessarily appropriate, educational exchange exists between the Philippines and the U.S. In medicine, for example, numbers of American doctors receive their schooling in the Philippines, where enrollment requirements are more lenient and costs are lower than in American medical schools. Conversely, a great number of Filipino nurses and doctors work in American hospitals in jobs which pay many times over what they do at home. This "brain drain" pattern can also be found in engineering, science, and other fields—and not just between the U.S. and the Philippines. Filipino training institutions are a national resource and a deserved point of pride, but a number of other countries become the beneficiaries as well.

As is often true elsewhere, university students in the Philippines are likely to display behavior and viewpoints which are atypical of the average person in the society. Political radicalism is strong, as is anti-Americanism. Filipino university students tend to be much more vocal, inquisitive, concerned, and politically active than are their parents or neighbors back home. The clothing considered acceptable for wear by women students, the relationships between men and women, and the social attitudes on campus would not go well in the barrio. Generally speaking, university students are also distinct from the average citizen because they tend to be drawn from families who can afford the tuition.

Even if campus life is not exactly mainstream, academic visitors to the Philippines enjoy a special advantage when it comes to understanding Filipino culture. For one thing, such visitors find themselves among English-speaking Filipinos who are educated and interested in their own culture. Studies and monographs on a wide variety of subjects relating to Filipino life and culture abound in the libraries. Filipino students and faculty are more informed about, and attuned to, American political and social developments than the average person. Given the natural hospitality of Filipinos, it would be rare for a foreign student or faculty member not to receive numerous invitations to visit villages and provinces, meet families, attend fiestas, or just go on outings. Such opportunities to see and learn firsthand and to practice one's language and cultural skills should not be passed up.

These special advantages don't come free, however. Academic visitors will likely find themselves with a lot of explaining to do. University students and faculty in the Philippines are urgently concerned about such issues as the future of the American military bases at Clark Field and Subic Bay, the movement of ships carrying nuclear weapons in and out of Philippine waters, the disastrously planned and eventually suspended billion-dollar Westinghouse project to build an atomic power plant in Bataan, the role of the

C.I.A. in internal Philippine political affairs, the impact of deci-sions in Washington on Philippine economic life and develop-ment, and, of course, the twenty years of American support for the dictatorship of Ferdinand and Imelda Marcos. American academic visitors would do well to go prepared to engage in debates and deal with attitudes which may not be a part of their normal field of interest.

Reaching Agreement

Americans going to the Philippines may find themselves in a number of situations where negotiations are required, whether they be for commercial, educational, or other objectives. Numer-ous variables enter into the picture, depending on the negotiator, whom he or she represents, the nature of the agreement being sought, and the circumstances requiring the negotiations. An American student trying to cajole a Filipino professor into allow-ing a make-up exam in the face of a failing grade at U.P. is in a different negotiating position from the owner of an American import firm looking for a supply of Baguio baskets. Coming to agreement on the price the U.S. should pay for maintaining its military bases in the Philippines is obviously a different exercise from that of an American college negotiating a study abroad arrangement at the University of Santo Thomas.

Given the array of factors affecting individual situations, are there any general considerations which an American might keep in mind in the negotiating process? The answer is yes, but what works in negotiating is much the same as what works in everyday situations, and the Filipino values and traits discussed in previous chapters come equally into play. We shall see how a sensitive regard for some of these are useful when Mr. Jones seeks agreement with Mr. Ramos.

Mr. Jones, our hypothetical American, is the head of Youth in Asia, a student travel organization. Having read the preceding chapters, Mr. Jones arrives in Manila with the objective of working out an agreement with Mr. Ramos, the owner of D'Tours, a Filipino travel agency. Mr. Jones has let Mr. Ramos know by letter that he is coming and would like to get together to discuss business. Because he is aware of the importance of establishing his own reputation and status and because he understands how significant personal relationships are in Filipino culture, Mr. Jones has mentioned in his letter to Mr. Ramos that their mutual friend, Mr. Santos, suggested that they get in touch. By using Mr. Santos's name, Mr. Jones can expect to be received as someone worthy of respect and consideration. He also knows that he owes a favor to Mr. Santos for being able to use his name in this way.

Mr. Ramos has been described to Mr. Jones as a somewhat conservative and traditional Filipino. While Filipinos in business often engage in matters with an American-like directness, Mr. Ramos is likely to respond better to a different approach. Rather than simply making a visit to Mr. Ramos's office, Mr. Jones calls him to suggest that they have lunch together. Aware that Filipinos enjoy social occasions and the process of developing contacts and friendships, Mr. Jones suggests a good restaurant and looks forward to a long and leisurely lunch. He dresses for the occasion in either a business suit or *barong tagalog*. Because he is the one asking for the meeting, Mr. Jones comes to the restaurant on time but is not disturbed when Mr. Ramos is late. Not only could the overwhelming Manila traffic cause a delay, but Mr. Ramos would also not want to be so punctual as to suggest that he might be desperate for Mr. Jones's business. When Mr. Ramos eventually arrives and apologizes for the delay, Mr. Jones assures him that he himself has just arrived.

Mr. Jones is careful not to plunge in with an exchange of first names; he lets Mr. Ramos set the pace. Later, when they have established a feeling of mutual regard and trust, Mr. Ramos tells Mr. Jones to call him "Ramon" and Mr. Jones is quick to respond with a similar invitation to call him "John."

Well aware of the need for this mutual relationship-building process to proceed comfortably, Jones makes no attempt to get down to business. He asks about Ramos's family and where he comes from in the Philippines. Each shows photographs of children and wife to the other. The conversation touches on their travels, the weather, and the news of the day. A few jokes are exchanged. Jones takes care to modulate his voice, keeping his tone friendly and quiet. He speaks at an easy pace, avoiding slang as well as forcefulness. As the meal progresses, one topic flows into another until, as if by mutual consent, it feels right to bring up the business interests which brought them together. Jones knew from the beginning that it would not happen until at least the soup course was finished.

At this point, Jones is considerably ahead of where he would have been had he arranged a meeting in Ramos's office and, in good American fashion, proceeded to say, "Well, I'll get right to the point. The reason I asked to see you..." In American terms, such an approach seems not only efficient but courteous as well since it conveys a respect for the other person's time. In Filipino terms, it feels like the proverbial cart before the horse. How can one negotiate or even discuss things seriously before knowing something of the person with whom one is talking?

When the lunch meeting comes to an end, Jones accepts the fact that no decisions have been reached and is not worried about it since Ramos has agreed to another meeting the next day. The relationship has been established and the negotiations are in process, though outwardly there is little to suggest that much progress has been made. Jones and Ramos now have a sense of what the other may want out of a possible arrangement, how eager each is to conclude an agreement, and how long the process may take before the sticking points are resolved. Jones pays the restaurant bill without a thought of suggesting to Ramos that they "go Dutch."

As he plans for the meeting the following day, Jones knows that when it comes to actual negotiations on details such as costs and division of labor, it will be important to maintain a relaxed and friendly atmosphere. Success will not come from putting Ramos into corners or pressuring him in a tone which suggests that he, the American, knows all the answers. Mr. Ramos's *amor-propio* must remain unthreatened and his views listened to respectfully. If agreement is difficult to reach, then Jones is aware that Ramos will be guided by a wish to find a compromise rather than to allow a win-lose situation to develop. In any event, their meeting must conclude on a light and pleasant note.

The negotiating process may well require more time than that allotted for their next encounter. Quite possibly, Ramos may invite Jones to dinner or suggest that he accompany him to a party to which he has been invited. Because it is important to Jones that D'Tours be the agency with which Youth in Asia works in the Philippines, he is prepared to let things proceed without undue pressure. He is confident that Ramos will be less interested in making an immediate profit than in establishing a working relationship which offers long-term prospects and potential rewards. Jones is prepared to accept his role in that process and knows that the relationship should not suddenly become impersonal after he returns home, just because he is no longer in the Philippines.

As They Are ...

Perhaps the most gratifying cross-cultural experience an American can have in the Philippines is to be among Filipinos who cease to feel it necessary to maintain a mask in front of the foreigner. On one memorable occasion the author brought three Filipino women together at his desk to discuss a problem among them. The meeting promised to consist of the usual, somewhat frustrating, indirect references to the disagreement, with polite assurances on everybody's part that "I'm only making a suggestion." Somewhat to his amazement, the author found himself in the middle of a frank, direct, and even heated debate. While never angry, the tone was clearly confrontational. Equally surprising, the three Filipinas were not looking for a referee or for a Solomon to render a decision on the matter. The discussion was an airing of concerns and issues. The unspoken message, left to the foreigner to decipher, was that the three women regarded him as a reference point in the dispute they were carrying on among themselves, trusting him to be able to understand more than one side of the story. If tempers flared and things were said without sugarcoating, that was all right too.

Such an occasion is not likely to happen often. When it does, the strains and setbacks which one has experienced in learning to understand and deal with another culture suddenly seem worth the effort. The differences which separate and the careful maintenance of correctness drop away.

Appendix 1

Critical Incidents

The incidents which follow focus on situations that commonly occur between Americans and Filipinos. In each, a difficult or a perplexing situation arises that requires you to decide on a course of action. Several choices are suggested for each situation, but one is preferable, that is, more likely to result in either improving the situation or at least not making it worse. While the encounters described in the critical incidents have not been specifically discussed in preceding chapters, the cultural elements which come into play have all been described previously. Working through these incidents provides you with an opportunity to review and test your understanding of Filipino cultural dynamics.

You may want to take the following approach. First, read each critical incident separately, along with the suggested options. Then make a choice and consider why that choice is preferable. Next, read the discussion section and compare your selected option with the one given. If they do not coincide, you may wish to review relevant sections of the text. Finally, go on to the next incident.

1—The Go-Between

An American branch manager, Jim, is dissatisfied with the work of a Filipino secretary. He calls her into his office and outlines the areas in which her work needs to improve. The next evening there is a company party, which he attends along with the Filipino office staff. While enjoying the party, Jim gets into a conversation with Alex, a Filipino who works in receiving and shipping. After some pleasantries and comments about the party are exchanged, Alex surprises Jim by mentioning the interview with the secretary the day before. Alex says that she happens to be from his home province and then tells him that the secretary feels terrible. Having been deliberately singled out and called into Jim's office, she feels so shamed in front of the other office workers that she is not sure she can continue with the company. Jim is astounded that the private conversation he held with the secretary would be a subject for comment by another staff member who had no part in the matter.

Options:

Jim should

A. tell Alex that personnel matters are private and not to be discussed with anyone but the individuals concerned,

B. find the secretary and warn her that Alex is trying to mind her business for her,

C. express regret that the secretary feels bad and change the subject, or

D. talk with Alex about his connection with the secretary.

Discussion:

Answer C will not get Jim into difficulty, but D would be the wiser action. Filipinos would not normally presume to talk to the manager about a fellow employee's work unless they (1) were invited to do so or (2) were acting in the capacity of go-between at the request of the employee concerned. Much of the Filipino quest for smooth interpersonal relations relies upon the good offices of go-betweens. From marriage proposals to professional favors to peacemaking, Filipino culture avoids face-to-face confrontation with its potential risk of loss of face, embarrassment, or violence. The intermediary plays an important role in making it possible for explanations, apologies, or indications of continuing goodwill to be passed between two parties who are temporarily estranged.

Jim should assume that Alex may have good reason to mention the secretary, particularly after he has offered a kind of legitimizing link between them involving a common provincial background. Rather than jump to conclusions, however, Jim should chat with Alex a bit to explore what his interest in the secretary might be. If it appears that Alex is truly acting as a go-between, then Jim might provide some explanation of his point of view about the secretary's work, with the comment that he hopes she will change her mind and stay with the company. Alex will soon deliver this message to the secretary, along with his own impressions of Jim's response. Even if the secretary continues for a time to be upset over having been called into Jim's office (with her colleagues aware of it), she will at least feel that her boss cares about her as a person.

2—Dinner

Susan works in an organization with Filipino colleagues. One of them, Lori, invites her to dinner at her house and Susan is pleased at the prospect. When she arrives at Lori's home, Susan finds that she is only one of a number of guests. She sits with the others, all Filipinos, and chats before dinner. Finally, Lori appears and announces that the meal is ready, with a special smile toward Susan. Knowing how busy Lori has been behind the scenes and wanting to show her appreciation, Susan gets up immediately and moves toward the dining room. She feels a little irritated by the lack of courtesy shown by the other guests, who simply sit and go on talking. As she is about to leave the living room, Susan becomes aware of a slight pause in the hum of conversation behind her. She sees some smiles and raised eyebrows directed her way.

Options:
Susan should

A. interpret the smiles and raised eyebrows as approval of her prompt courtesy to the hostess by leading the way to the table,

B. assume that she is the center of attention only because she is a foreigner, or

C. ask herself if she is doing something wrong and find a pretext to change her direction away from the dining room.

Discussion:

The smart thing for Susan is to be aware that she is doing something which causes amusement among the Filipinos. Their smiles and raised eyebrows will not be disapproving but merely ironic and playful, and Susan needs to be sensitive to the nuances of the moment. She should strike up a conversation with someone nearby or head for the bathroom, as if that were what she intended to do when she got up. In Filipino culture, someone who jumps up to get to the table when dinner is announced is displaying the manners of a glutton or child. Urging is required of the guests, who only reluctantly—as if their enjoyment were not really dependent upon food—make their way to the table. Getting there later is certainly better than being first, but any foreign guests in the house will usually be urged to the table ahead of others.

3—Gossip

George is an American coordinator of a project employing Filipino staff. It seems to him that one of the daily occupations of the Filipinos is the trading of tsismis, or gossip, which he finds very childish and irritating. One day Raul comes to him and manages to work into the conversation a reference to Ramon, George's foreman, letting George know indirectly that Ramon has been falsifying the purchase orders and taking kickbacks from suppliers.

Options:

George should

A. do some private checking on Ramon,

B. tell Raul that gossip is not worthy of a professional, or

C. explain to Raul that he prefers not to get involved in rumors and gossip.

Discussion:

Choice A would be the wisest. Tsismis is a fact of life in Filipino society—one which Filipinos often decry, but one about which they can be quite sensitive when criticized. Jealousy and malice lie behind a great deal of petty gossip. Sometimes, however, tsismis is motivated by more honorable concerns. Where direct confrontation is culturally not possible, gossip may be a means through which people express their outrage or their distaste for the behavior of others. The fact that "there are 'talks' about it" (in Filipino phraseology) soon gets back to the ears of the offending person, who either corrects the behavior or accepts the risks of public displeasure.

George would do well not to dismiss what Raul tells him out of hand but to file it away mentally. It may be no more than idle rumormongering, or it may be Raul's way of letting him know indirectly that Ramon is involved in improprieties. Perhaps it is Raul's way of warning Ramon to stop whatever he is doing before it is too late. It can also be a malicious attempt to discredit Ramon and get rid of him. As always, one needs to be alert.

4—Language

Roger works closely with a group of Filipinos on an agricultural development project. Since he does not speak Tagalog, he uses English in all his interactions with his colleagues. When the Filipinos are conversing together, they speak in Tagalog. Normally that does not bother Roger, except when they carry on a Tagalog conversation in front of him. He does not say anything about it, but it continues to irritate him since he feels that he is being deliberately excluded. One day, while Roger and the Filipinos are speaking in English together, something is said in Tagalog and for the next five minutes all the Filipinos leave the English language and the American listener behind. Roger, meanwhile, is offended at suddenly being dropped from the conversation and kept in the dark about what the Filipinos find so interesting.

Options:

Roger should

A. assert himself and insist on everyone speaking English when he is present,

B. just wait patiently until the Filipinos resume speaking in English, or

C. walk away to let his colleagues know that he is displeased.

Discussion:

Roger should take option B. He might also make a good-humored appeal for everyone to return to English. He could even try to learn Tagalog. As frustrating or irritating as the situation may be, Roger should not let himself be offended or angry. The Filipinos may be deliberately excluding him from the conversation—for reasons specific to that occasion—or they may simply be reverting to Tagalog because it allows them to communicate easily with each other. Quite often this slipping from Tagalog to English and back again happens without Filipinos even being aware of it. Sliding back into Tagalog, Cebuano, or any other indigenous language may also occur out of pure fatigue from the strain of speaking English. Normally, Filipinos are courteous and considerate of the foreigner's lack of understanding of the local languages and do their best to communicate in English.

5—Right Answer

Becky is an experienced American educator who works in a program training Filipino teachers of English. After observing their teaching for two weeks, she decides that the Filipino teachers are too focused upon their repertoire of classroom techniques. Becky feels that while the teachers are quite expert in handling the techniques they employ, they use them indiscriminately simply because they have learned them. She is sure that the Filipinos would benefit from having a better understanding of educational principles, so that they might select techniques from a number of options, depending on the particular needs and circumstances of a lesson. Becky organizes a special training session. She first discusses several educational principles which will come into play in the lesson she will demonstrate. She tells the teacher trainees that she will teach the same lesson three times, using a different technique each time. She stresses that the trainees should focus on the educational principles involved and should see that the choice of technique is a matter of judgment and personal decision. After finishing the three sample lessons, Becky asks if there are any questions. One trainee raises her hand and asks, "Which one is right?"

Options:
Becky should
A. reprimand the trainee for not paying attention,
B. remind the trainees of the purpose of her demonstration lessons, or
C. discuss how the question reflects the Filipino mentality regarding rote learning and the source of authority.

Discussion:
Becky should expect such a question to be asked, particularly if among the trainees there are older Filipinos or those coming from rural and village backgrounds. There is no reason, however, for her to abandon her lesson goals. The best response is B. Becky should consider first that she may not have been as clear as she thought in explaining the aim of the demonstration lessons. She should repeat the objective of the session, pointing out that the choice of classroom techniques may be "right" or "wrong" depending upon particular circumstances. Most likely, among the trainees there are several who comprehended the lesson objective quite well. Becky should draw them into the discussion by asking them to explain the principles she tried to impart. In this way Becky reinforces her main point, the validity of individual judgment.

6—Giving a Gift

Harry is invited to the home of a Filipino friend for dinner. Wanting to show his appreciation, he spends some time finding a rather elegant gift to present to the hostess. He is pleased with it and feels sure it will be appreciated by his hosts. When he arrives for the occasion and is welcomed inside, Harry presents the beautifully wrapped gift to the lady of the house. Instead of opening it, she chides him pleasantly for "taking the trouble" and then lays it aside on the hallway table.

Options:
Harry should
A. conclude that he has erred and that it is not appropriate to present a gift to a dinner hostess,
B. mention the gift and suggest that the hostess might like to open it, or
C. enjoy the evening and not refer to the gift.

Discussion:
Harry has done the right thing in bringing the gift, and his best response is C, to enjoy the evening. In opening the gift in front of him, the hostess would appear to be either greedy or needy and thus lacking *delicadesa*, and she would risk embarrassing Harry by openly displaying the gift's value. It is far more important for the hostess to show appreciation for the act of giving on Harry's part than to show too much concern over the gift itself. After Harry has gone, she will open the gift and gratefully remember who gave it to her. She may thank Harry by mentioning the gift on some occasion a few days later. In any event, the gift represents a bond between Harry and the family—one which, appropriately and in due time, will be reciprocated.

7—House Blessing

Celia, an American, manages an operation in Cebu employing a number of Filipinos. One of her section chiefs, Dominico, has built a new home for his parents and relatives in the country and invites her to attend the house blessing, which will be held on a Sunday in about two weeks. While she appreciates the invitation, Celia is not pleased at the prospect of having to spend a whole Sunday getting to and from the remote village where Dominico's parents live. Besides, she already has plans for that day anyway. She explains this to Dominico, but he simply brushes aside her reason and replies, "You must come." A few days later Dominico reminds her of the house blessing. Celia again tells him that she unfortunately has other plans and extends her best wishes for the occasion. Dominico replies, "You'll be there."

Options:

Celia should

A. tell Dominico that she will try to attend the house blessing,

B. make it clear to Dominico that she cannot come so that he does not have any false expectations, or

C. attend the house blessing.

Discussion:

The best choice for Celia is A: tell Dominico that she will try to attend. The worst thing she can do is to refuse the invitation. Honesty, in this case, is not the best policy. Dominico's family will be receiving a number of guests for the house blessing. He will be very pleased if his American boss shows up, but if she does not, there are any number of reasons which may have prevented her from attending, from illness to a flat tire, just as there are reasons why other invited guests may not be able to get there. Employing American ideas of what is honest and forthright in this situation simply leads to hard feelings. Dominico will take any direct refusal of the invitation as a personal slight. He will take a promise to "try to get there" in the same way he expects others to take his own promises of good intentions. When, later, Celia apologizes for the inopportune total breakdown of her car's engine and expresses interest in how the house blessing went and her regrets for missing it, Dominico's amor-propio remains intact, whatever he may privately believe about her excuse.

8—*Bad Turn*

An American professor, Mary, has a number of Filipino acquaintances among those teaching in her department. One evening she gives a ride into town to Lourdes, a Filipina with a Ph.D. and a number of scholarly works to her credit. As they come to a sharp turn in the road, Mary notices Lourdes unself-consciously crossing herself. Intrigued, Mary asks her faculty colleague why she felt the need to make the sign of the cross. Lourdes replies that there was an accident at this curve the year before and there may be uneasy spirits at the place. After more questioning, Mary learns that Lourdes thinks the ghost of the driver killed in the accident might still haunt the scene.

Options:
Mary should
A. accept the statement and drive on into town,
B. tease Lourdes out of her superstitious ideas, or
C. explain rationally to Lourdes why the combination of superstition and education seem contradictory.

Discussion:
Mary's best choice is to drive on into town. Americans may find it surprising that Filipinos have no problem in combining a Western orientation with what, in American cultural terms, are normally considered to be superstitious beliefs. Ghosts, tree spirits, elves, old-men-on-anthills (tiny dwarfs who wear white hats if they are good and black hats if they are not), and other denizens of the paranormal abound in common Filipino thinking. There are Filipinos who scoff at the whole thing. There are more, however, who continue to believe in the occult to one degree or another, even as they adhere otherwise to quite conventional ideas of science and religion.

There would be no harm in discussing the matter with Lourdes, as long as Mary can do so without passing judgment. Most likely, Lourdes will be highly interested in the subject, and Mary will learn something more about Filipino culture.

9—White Face

Kevin is an American attending a weekend seminar along with a number of Filipino salesmen. They are accommodated in a wing of the conference center. Many complaints are heard up and down the halls since the air-conditioning seems to be off and the evening is very hot. Kevin's Filipino roommate goes to the dormitory clerk to tell him to turn on the cooling system. After thirty minutes no change is evident. At that point the roommate expresses his frustration and says to Kevin, "Go show him your white face, and he'll turn the air-con on."

Options:

Kevin should

A. explain to his roommate that he is just a participant at the seminar and has no special authority,

B. go talk to the dormitory clerk and see if he can get the air-conditioning turned on, or

C. refuse the suggestion on the grounds that it smacks of racism.

Discussion:

Kevin's best course of action is to go talk to the clerk about getting the air-conditioning on. At least that will accomplish something useful. Protests about his lack of authority will not change the Filipino disposition to respect foreign white skin more than native brown. Despite a growing awareness and self-esteem on the part of Filipinos toward themselves and the Filipino culture, centuries of colonialism still have their effect. Kevin's authority is conferred upon him, whether he wants it or not, by Filipinos still influenced by a history in which whiteness and power went together. If he sticks to his principles and refuses to talk to the clerk on racial grounds, his roommate would certainly understand and maybe even admire that stance. Meanwhile, however, he and the other Filipinos would still have to suffer through a hot and uncomfortable night, and Kevin's Filipino colleagues might well resent his refusal to help them.

Appendix 2

Language and Words

I. Pilipino words often encountered by travelers and residents, either in writing or speech:

adobo   -   popular stew made of chicken and/or pork, garlic, soy sauce, and vinegar.

aling   -   prefix of respect for a mature woman. Usage will often include the cleaning lady or other person of low status to soften the distinctions of class.

amor-propio -   self-respect, pride in oneself, "face."

barangay   -   village or small section of a town.

barkada   -   group, peer group, set, fellows, playmates, "batch."

barong   -   the Filipino national dress for men—a shirt worn outside the trousers. A long-sleeved, decorated version worn on formal occasions is known as a *barong tagalog*; the short-sleeved style is often referred to as a "sports barong."

barrio - village or small section of a town.

bundok - mountain. While this word may not be one the traveler hears frequently, the American will recognize it in its English-language idiomatic form: "boondock(s)."

delicadesa - delicacy, sensitivity or appropriateness of manner.

despedida - a going-away party.

hindi - no.

hiya - shame/propriety/guilt—according to context.

lavandera - a washerwoman.

lechon - a whole roast pig or piglet.

Malacanang - the presidential palace.

mang - prefix of respect for a mature man (see *aling*).

merienda - the usual word for "snack." It could be a morning, an afternoon, or even a midnight merienda. To Americans, the size of a merienda may look like a whole meal-between-meals. Filipinos sometimes joke about their own interest in eating, saying, "After we finish breakfast, we start thinking about lunch."

na (na lang) - see "already" in the English list. Although na is defined in the dictionary as "already," it has many meanings. It is one of those Pilipino words often mixed into English sentences. For example, the answer to the question "What film do you want to see—this one here or the one across town?" might be "This one, na lang," meaning "Let's just see this one" (and not make the trip across town). Lang often conveys a slightly dismissing or diminishing quality, as in "OK na lang," which has the meaning of "I'm (sort of) fine."

oo   -   yes (pronounced as a short "oh").

pakikisama   -   a sociological term referring to concession, getting along, going along with the crowd's wishes, accommodating to the group in order to be accepted.

pansit   -   a common noodle dish.

pasalubong   -   gifts which the traveler brings back to those at home.

pinoy   -   colloquial for a Filipino.

salamat   -   thanks, thank you.

sige   -   OK, yes, of course, etc. Sige (pronounced "sigay") has various meanings, depending on the context. Sige na, for example, can mean "Let's do it," as in "Do you want to go for a walk?" "Sige na!" (Sure! Why not?)

tio, tita   -   uncle, aunt.

tsismis   -   gossip.

utang na loob   -   recognition of a debt, exchanging favors, knowing one's self to be obligated.

II. English words used differently or more frequently in the Philippines than in the U.S.:

(Generally, in languages of the Philippines, the next-to-last syllable is stressed. This pattern often carries over into English and can make immediate understanding difficult for the American, even if the grammar and vocabulary of the utterance are completely correct.)

already - now, just. "I already want to go" does not mean, "After hearing about the wonders of the place, I have quickly decided I want to go there." More likely it means, "I'm ready to leave now (this place, this party, etc.)." "Already" is the schoolbook translation of the particle *na*. Na, however, has numerous meanings, depending on context, and thus the American may hear an "already" in a sentence in a place he or she would not use it, or hear it in the right place but with a different meaning than the native speaker would give to the statement. The English word *just* will often be the better translation; for example, "Let's eat already" means "Let's just go ahead and eat (and not wait for her to get here)."

also - "either" in negative contexts. For example, "She isn't going also" is the Filipino way of saying, "She isn't going either."

batch - a group of people rather than an aggregate of substances. For example, "She was in my batch when I enrolled."

blow-out - a party, ranging from a beer shared by two friends to a full-scale social event; a treat offered to a friend or friends by someone who has reason to celebrate.

brownout - a term which probably came from days when the electricity may have merely dimmed. Today, a brownout means a total loss of power.

go down - get off. "Do we go down here?" means, "Do we get off the bus here?"

gossips (and other plurals) - "There were a lot of gossips about her at the time." Most likely, the speaker does not mean that several gossiping people were gathered around the person concerned but that multiple items of gossip were being spread. This is generally a problem of differentiating between count (apple, table, opinion) and noncount (gossip, information, milk) nouns.

green - off-color. Where Americans have blue movies and dirty jokes, Filipinos have blue movies and green jokes. "He liked to tell dark green jokes."

jeepney - While this is not really an English word, it derives from the trademark Jeep and refers to a popular form of local transportation involving a jeep-style vehicle carrying passengers in the rear.

meet an accident - In the U.S. people "have" an accident. In the Philippines, people "meet" an accident.

orig   -   colloquial for "original," that is, a U.S. citizen by birth as opposed to a Filipino naturalized citizen of the United States.

pass   -   go by or go via. "He passed by Manila" means "He went via Manila"; "Let's pass this way" means "Let's go this route"; and "Don't forget to pass by the store on your way home" means "Don't forget to stop at the store on your way home."

salvage/
salvaging   -   the common term for the abduction and subsequent disappearance/murder of persons by either official or resistance forces.

she/he   -   Indigenous languages in the Philippines have one word for both *he* and *she*, as do a number of other languages around the world. Thus, Filipinos often mix up the gender pronouns: "I spoke with Ramon and she said ..." or "Maria is an important person in the office. Nothing would get done without him." The mix-up of gender in a short sentence can easily be accommodated by the American listener. In a longer exchange, when the "hes" and "shes" seem to be floating aimlessly, Americans tend to feel a high degree of anxiety because they are confused. The best response is to ask for clarification.

viand   -   anything that goes with rice, referring often to vegetables. "Don't you want any viand to eat?"

Resources

Any traveler to the Philippines can find an abundance of works on Filipino life, culture, art, and other topics, many of them written in English.

Considerable research on social, cultural, historical, and artistic aspects of life in the Philippines is published by Filipino scholars and writers. American scholarly and journalistic attention to the Philippines has continued for decades, and any good public library or bookstore will have a supply of titles. A personal interest in a given topic makes a fine place to start since the variety and number of works about Filipinos and the Philippines are so great that it is difficult to select just a few for special mention.

Learning how Filipinos see themselves can be one of the most useful ways to understand the culture. In addition to sociological or cultural studies, Filipino fiction provides a subtle insight into their values, customs, and behavior. Filipino writers often write in English as well as in their native language. English translations of works written in one of the major local languages can also be found.

Foreign-published books are costly in the Philippines, while locally produced works are relatively inexpensive. Bookstores are numerous in Manila and in several other large cities. A tour through the Quiapo (a section of Manila) branch of National Bookstores will provide an eye-opening experience in terms of the sheer breadth of what is available and also some insight into Filipino reading preferences.

Here are a few titles by way of a start. For the traveler with little reading time available, two of the following works will be of particular interest. Stanley Karnow's *In Our Image: America's Empire in the Philippines* provides a detailed explanation of American-Philippine historical and contemporary relations. Alfredo and Grace Roces's *Culture Shock! Philippines* offers a number of useful perspectives on Filipino culture along with practical dos and don'ts for visitors and travelers.

* * * *

Paraluman S. Aspillera. *Basic Tagalog*. Manila: M.& L. Licudine Ent., 1981.

A grammar for both "foreigners and non-Tagalogs" by the founder of the Institute of Filipino Language and Culture. This work, along with a native-speaking instructor, would serve the reader well in gaining a good understanding of the language which forms the basis of the national language, Pilipino.

Leonard Casper. *New Writing from the Philippines: A Critique and Anthology*. Syracuse: Syracuse University Press, 1966.

Topics such as traditional folk patterns and values, efforts by Filipino writers to define unifying elements of Filipino culture beyond class distinctions, the historical context in which Filipino literature has developed, and a selection of Filipino poems, stories, and drama are all included in this large book.

James Fenton. "The Snap Revolution: James Fenton in the Philippines." *Granta* 18 (1987).

A collection of articles centering on the overthrow of the Marcos regime, providing insights into contemporary Filipino life and values.

Stanley Karnow. *In Our Image: America's Empire in the Philippines*. New York: Random House, 1989.

A comprehensive survey of U.S.-Philippine relations, from

America's almost accidental involvement in the Philippines in 1898 to the present. The work combines historical research and contemporary journalism into what will remain for some time the best single source on the tangled, emotional, and often tragic relationship between the two countries.

Carl H. Lande, ed. *Rebuilding a Nation: Philippine Challenges and American Policy.* Washington, D.C.: Washington Institute Press, 1987.
A collection of thirty-two articles on Philippine history, economy, government and politics, and U.S. policy.

Raul S. Manglapus. *Will of the People: Original Democracy in Non-Western Societies.* New York: Freedom House, 1987.
This work traces the roots of consensus government in traditional societies around the world, prior to the advent of Western concepts and forms of democracy, including discussion of the early Filipino-Malay *adat* (pre-European customs, laws, and procedures governing societal interaction).

Donald E. McQuinn. *Wake in Darkness.* New York: Tom Doherty Associates, 1984.
Just for contrast, a spy thriller set in almost-contemporary Philippines. Through the adventures of a deep-cover CIA agent, with a spicy mixture of conspiracy, corruption, violence, and madness, the writer offers a more sympathetic insight into Filipino culture than might be expected.

Alfredo and Grace Roces. *Culture Shock! Philippines.* Singapore: Times Books International, 1985.
An excellent survey of contemporary Filipino culture, with particular focus on practical dos and don'ts for the foreigner expecting to live and work in the country. Topics include Filipino cultural values, business and social etiquette, Filipino fiestas, history, and practical matters such as finding a maid or renting a house.

Bienvenido N. Santos. *The Man Who (Thought He) Looked Like Robert Taylor*. Quezon City: New Day Publishers, 1983.

The fourth novel of a Filipino writer living in the United States. Santos's theme in this truly cross-cultural work is the poignancy of homelessness experienced by the Filipino who may live in the U.S. for years but always feels that someday he will return home to the islands.

Daniel B. Schirmer & Stephen Rosskamm Shalom, eds. *The Philippines Reader: A History of Colonialism, Neocolonialism, Dictatorship, and Resistance*. Boston: South End Press, 1987.

Readings and documents from the earliest American involvement in the Philippines to the present. Items include official government papers, editorials, manifestos, articles, and letters from U. S. and Filipino sources.

Leon Wolff. *Little Brown Brother*. New York: Doubleday & Co., Inc., 1960.

A readable and sympathetic account of "How the Americans Conquered the Philippines in 1898-1902." Wolff provides an informative view of American attitudes at the turn of the century and of events and personalities in the Philippines which led to confrontation and conquest. The work was banned under the Marcos regime for its uncomplimentary view of U.S. intervention.